AUTHENTIC TRANSCRIPTIONS
WITH NOTES AND TABLATURE

The Best of Janis Joplin

Music transcriptions by Jeff Jacobson and Paul Pappas

Cover photo by Jim Cummins/STAR FILE
Used by permission

ISBN 0-7935-9807-9

7777 W. Bluemound Rd. P.O. Box 13819 Milwaukee, WI 53213

Visit Hal Leonard Online at
www.halleonard.com

Photo courtesy of Laura Joplin

Contents

Janis Joplin By Laura Joplin

Janis Lynn Joplin was born January 19, 1943 and died October 4, 1970. In between, she led a triumphant and tumultuous life blessed by an innate talent to convey powerful emotion through heart-stomping rock and roll. Born and raised in Southeast Texas, Janis broke from social customs during the tense days of racial integration, standing up for the rights of African Americans whose segregated status in her hometown seared her youthful ideals. Along with a fellow group of beatnik-reading high school students, she pursued the non-traditional via the arts — especially music. Discovering a talent to belt the blues, Janis copied the styles of Bessie Smith, Odetta, Mahalia Jackson, and Leadbelly. She played the coffee houses in the small towns of Texas, ventured to the beatnik haunts of Venice, eventually pausing for a year in Austin as a student at the University of Texas. Jumping into the passionate lifestyle cultivated by the beats, Janis thrilled at her creativity. During her later stays in North Beach and the Village in New York she almost lost herself in her experiments with drugs and alcohol.

Photo by John Byrne Cooke

In 1965 she returned home for a year to get clean, question her life direction and possibly marry. She excelled at college but was never content. Music still called to her in spite of its dangers of association with drugs and alcohol. As the marriage plans fell through, Austin friend Chet Helms called offering a singing position in a relatively obscure new San Francisco group called Big Brother and the Holding Company. Janis found a home of the heart. Big Brother played in the Bay area to increasing enthusiasm for their unique brand of psychedelic rock. The group signed with Mainstream Records, a small outfit that produced a poorly promoted album and two singles, "Blindman" and "All Is Loneliness." Then in the summer of 1967 Big Brother played the Monterey International Pop Festival and Janis claimed the public spotlight with Big Mama Thornton's "Ball and Chain."

Photo by Elliott Landy/STAR FILE

Courted by manager powerhouse, Albert Grossman, the band signed a new deal with Columbia Records. Their *Cheap Thrills* album was released in August of 1968 and soon went gold, introducing the hits "Piece of My Heart" and "Summertime." The band was playing to large audiences for big fees, and the billing now read "Janis Joplin with Big Brother and the Holding Company." The pressure mounted, the income rose, and the hippie

Photo by John Byrne Cooke

rockers could afford higher priced drugs. Their experimenting escalated and soon heroin was popular in their social crowd. The band's performing and work relations soured, and on December 1, 1968 they played their last gig together.

Going solo, Janis returned to her love of blues, releasing the album *I Got Dem Ol' Kozmic Blues Again Mama!* in September of 1969. While the American counterculture press chastised her for leaving Big Brother, European audiences welcomed the group with foot-stomping accolades. The Charges of abandoning her San Francisco roots hurt Janis and prevented the group from receiving the attention its musical greatness deserved. Janis seemed to court public attention by upping the daring in her anything-goes lifestyle. Her antics grew increasingly risky. Finally recognizing the drug problem, Janis began trying to quit.

In 1970, Janis formed a third group, The Full Tilt Boogie Band. They embodied a new mix of rock and blues, crafting a more unique "Joplin" sound to support her. Janis was never happier with her new music and the members of the group. While recording her next album, *Pearl*, she unfortunately sampled an extra-pure dose of heroin, dying at the age of 27. Her third album was released posthumously to wide acclaim, launching the popular songs "Me and Bobby McGee" and "Mercedes Benz."

Decades after her death, Janis commands a growing popularity. Famous for her lifestyle and her music, Janis Joplin speaks to Boomers from the 1960s and a new group of younger loyalists, reaching across time with heart-felt declarations like, "You gotta be true to yourself, 'cause your *self* is all you really got in life."

Photo by Jim Cummins/STAR FILE

from *Janis Joplin's Greatest Hits*

Ball and Chain

Words and Music by Willie Mae (Big Mama) Thornton

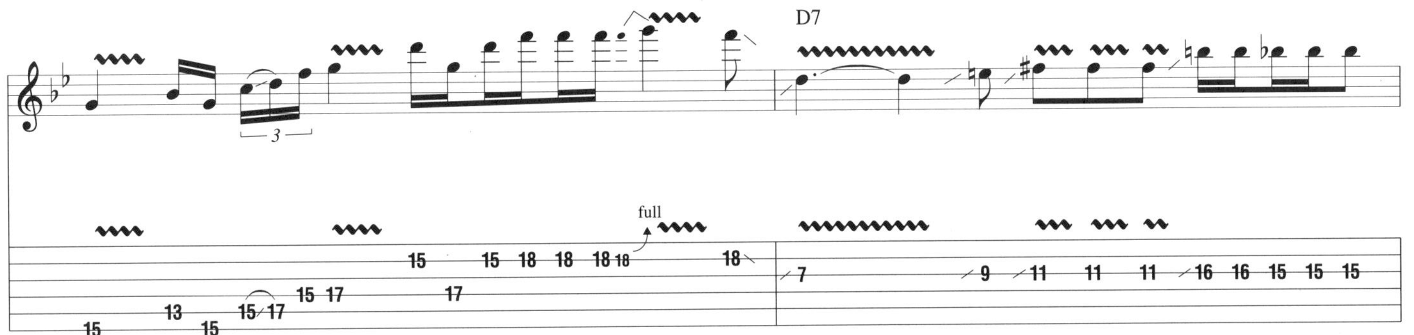
D7
full

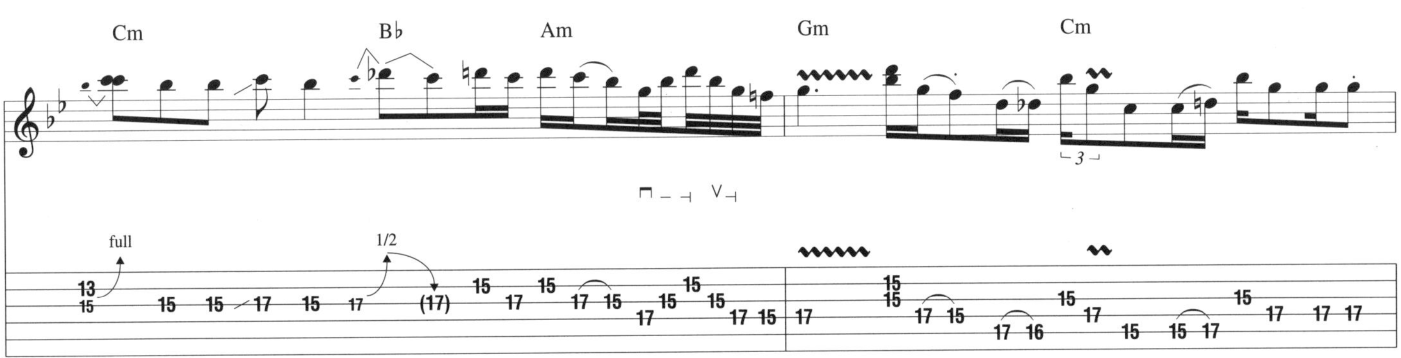
Cm
B♭
Am
Gm
Cm
full
1/2

D7#9
Verse
Gm
1. S - sit-tin' down by my win -
fdbk.
mf
w/ clean tone
1/4

Cm7
Gtr. 1 tacet
Gm7
dow, hon-ey oh, look-in' out at the rain.
Gtr. 1
Gtr. 2
* Gtr. 2
divisi
mp
* Piano arr. for gtr.

Cm
S - sit-tin' down by _ me in my win -
dow, Lord-y. ___ All a-round I felt it.
Gm7
All I could see was-a rain. ___
Dm7
Some-thing grabbed a - hold of me, hon-ey. Felt to me, ___
Cm7
B♭
Am
Gtr. 2 tacet
Gm
Cm
hon-ey, like, _ Lord, ___ a ball and chain. ___ Yeah, _ hey. ___ You know what I mean.
Gtr. 2
Gtr. 1
divisi
w/ dist.
Gtr. 1
let ring

D7#9
When it's way too heav - y for you, you can't hold it no more. Say
Chorus
Gm
Cm
whoa, oh, whoa, oh. Hon-ey, this can't be just be-cause I got - ta want your love. Please, please,
whoa, oh, whoa, oh. Hon-ey, this can't be not an - y-thing I ev - er want-ed from you, dad-dy. Tell me, nah, nah,
simile on repeat
Gm
please, please. Whoa, please, please.
nah, nah. Oh, tell me, nah, yeah. I say,
1/4
Cm
Whoa, oh, whoa, oh, hon-ey, this can't be just be - cause I got - ta need you, dad - dy. Please,
whoa, oh, whoa, oh, hon-ey, this can't be. Nah, nah, nah, nah, nah, nah, nah, nah, nah, nah, nah, nah, nah, nah, nah, nah,

To Coda
Gm
don't you let me down now.
nah, nah, nah, nah, nah, nah, nah, nah, nah, nah.
Please, yeah.
Yeah, yeah, yeah. Yeah.
1/4
D7
Cm
B♭
Am
Hey, you're gone to-day. Hon-ey, I want-ed to love you. I want-ed to hold ya, yeah, till the day I die.
Gm
Cm
D
Yes, I did. Yes, I did. Yeah, hey, hey, all right.
Guitar Solo
Gm
Cm
full
1/2
1 1/2

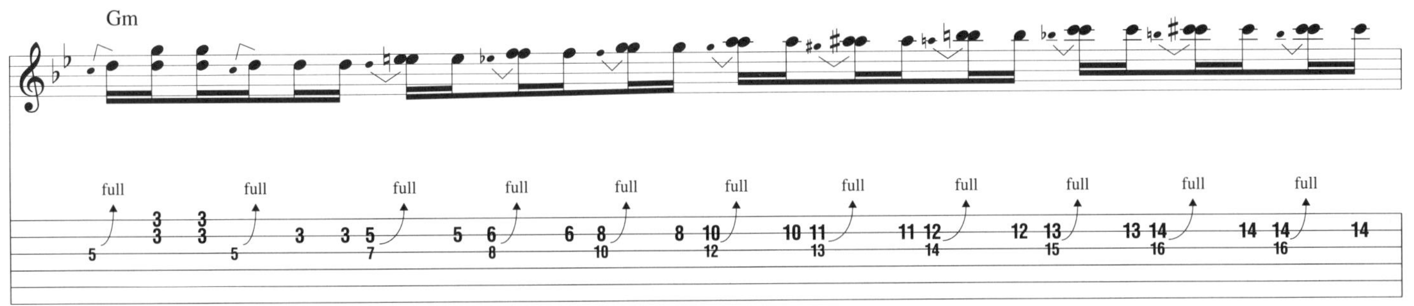

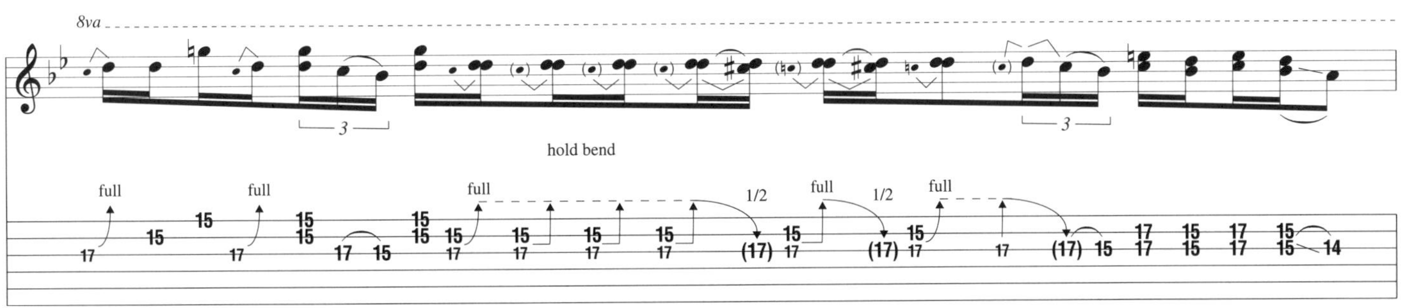

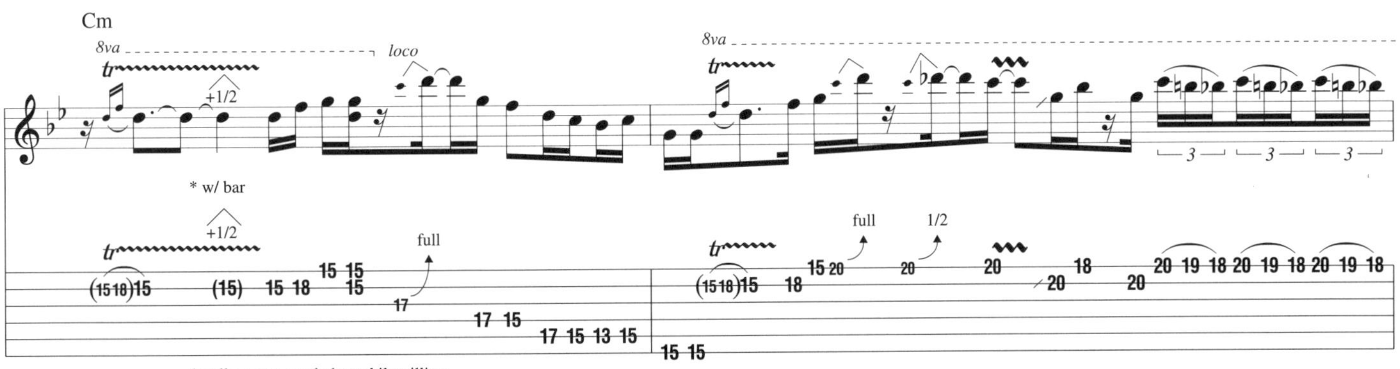

* pull up on tremolo bar while trilling.

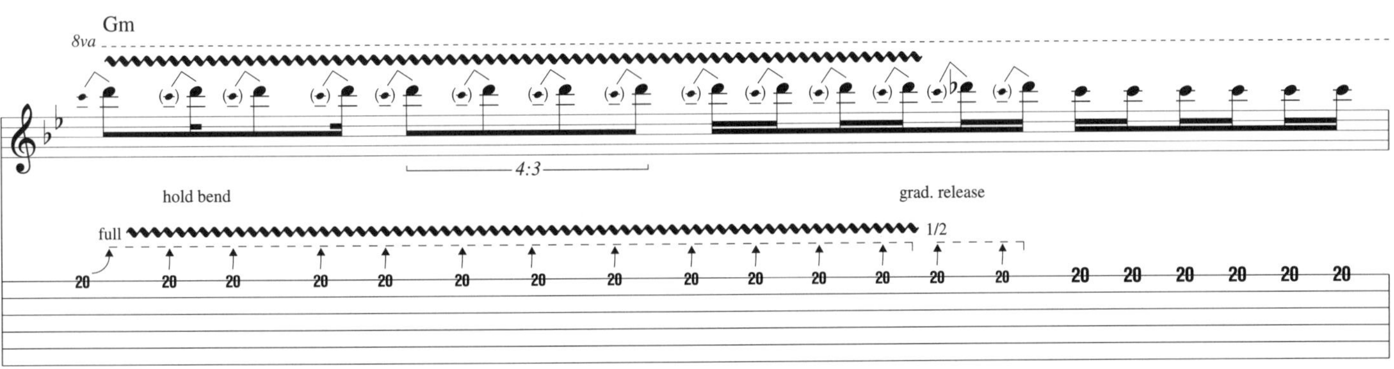

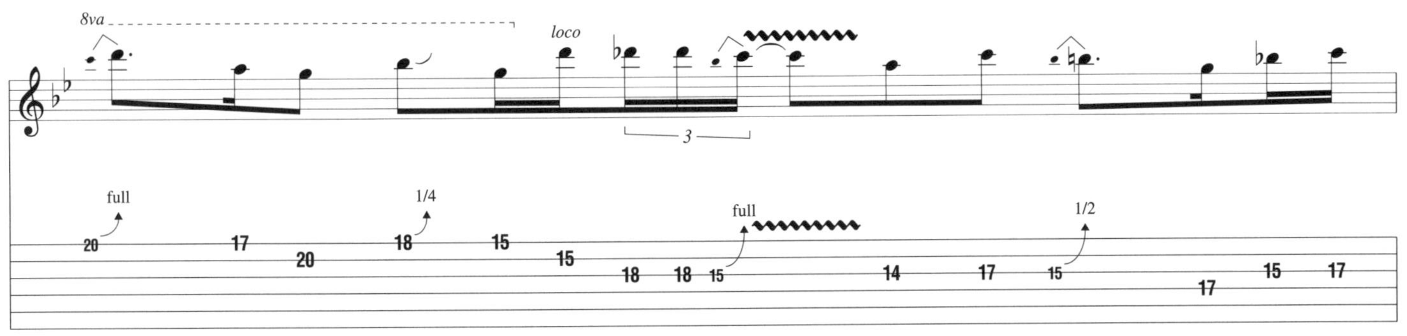

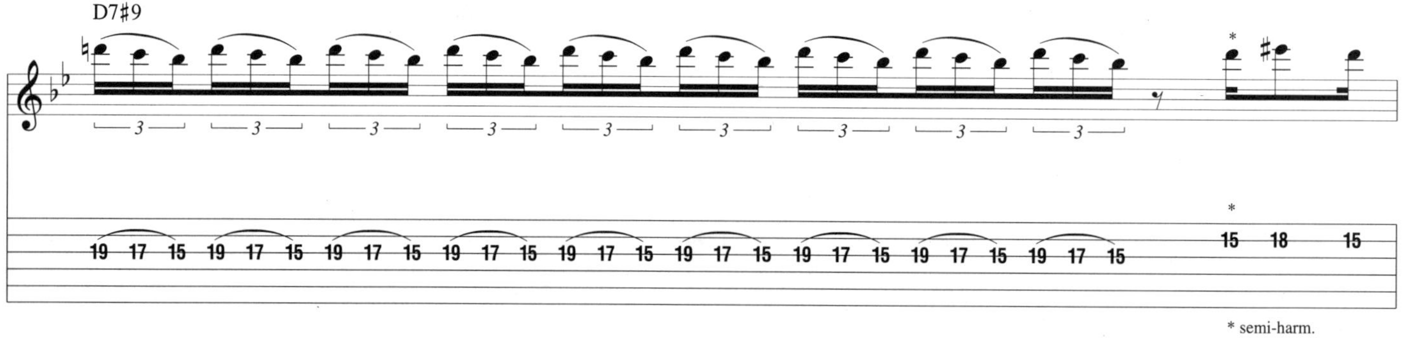
D7♯9
* semi-harm.

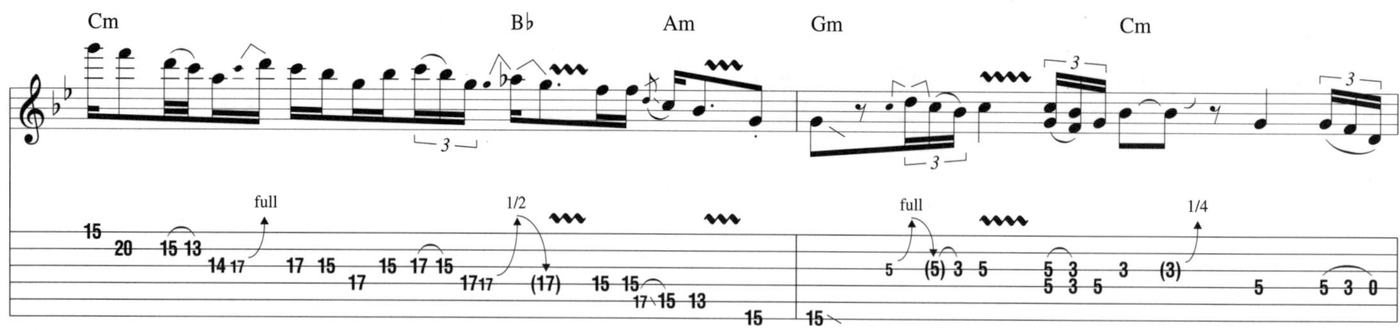
Cm
B♭
Am
Gm
Cm
full
1/2
full
1/4

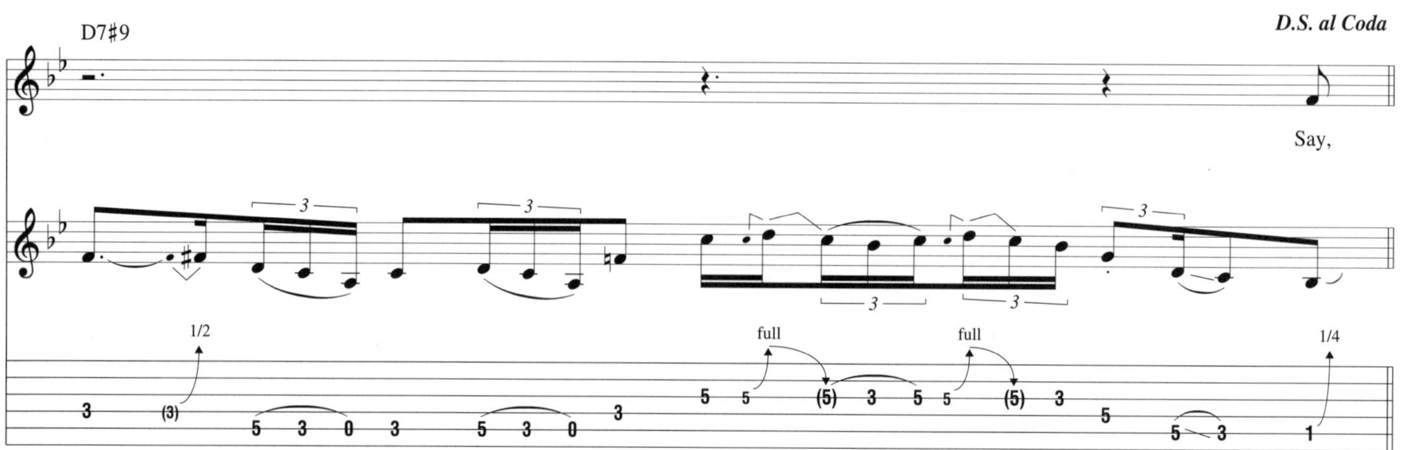
D7♯9
D.S. al Coda
Say,
1/2
full
full
1/4

Coda
D7♯9
Free Time
Cm N.C.
10:6
I, ba-by, want some-one if they could tell me, tell me, why. Just be-cause I got-ta
w/ clean tone

want your love. Hon-ey, just be-cause I got-ta need, need, need your love.

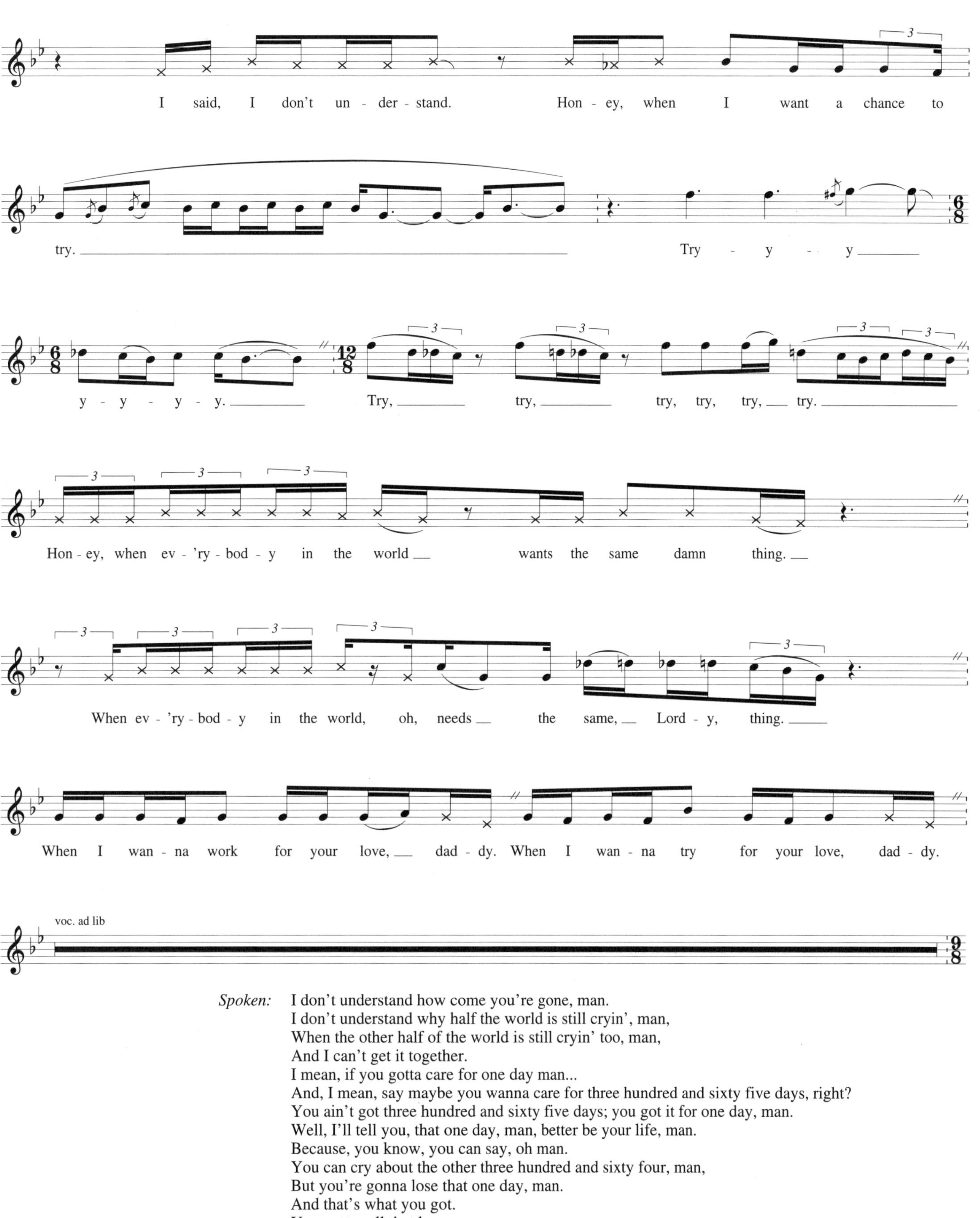

Spoken: I don't understand how come you're gone, man.
I don't understand why half the world is still cryin', man,
When the other half of the world is still cryin' too, man,
And I can't get it together.
I mean, if you gotta care for one day man...
And, I mean, say maybe you wanna care for three hundred and sixty five days, right?
You ain't got three hundred and sixty five days; you got it for one day, man.
Well, I'll tell you, that one day, man, better be your life, man.
Because, you know, you can say, oh man.
You can cry about the other three hundred and sixty four, man,
But you're gonna lose that one day, man.
And that's what you got.
You gotta call that love, man.
That's what it is, man.
If you got a today, you don't wear it tomorrow, man.
'Cause you don't need it.
'Cause, as a matter of fact, as we discovered on the train,
Tomorrow never happens, man.
It's all the same fucking day, man.

So, you got - ta, when you wan - na hold some - bod - y,

you got - ta hold 'em like it's the last min - ute of your life. You got - ta
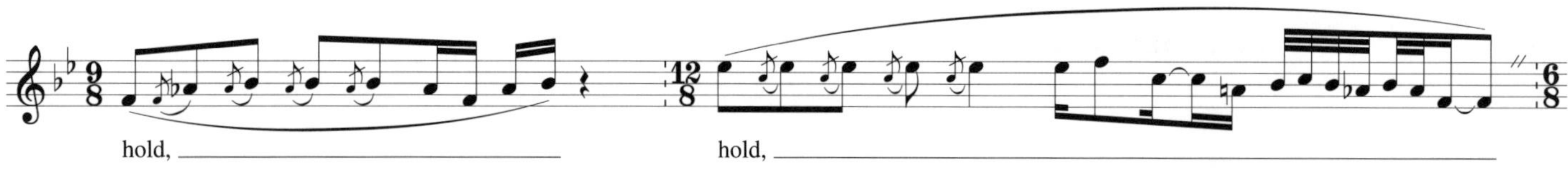
hold,
hold,

hold.

Hold it,
'cause some-day, some weight gon - na come on your should-ers, babe. It's gon - na

feel too heav - y. It's gon - na weigh on ya. It's gon - na feel just like a

ball,
ball,

ball,
oh, dad - dy and a

chain.

from *Pearl*

Cry Baby

Words and Music by Norman Meade and Bert Russell

To Coda
Verse
Am
G
C
ah.
seem to do,
1. I know she tell
2. Don't you know,
mf
let ring
F
G6
F6/G
ya,
hon', I know she told you that she loves you much
hon-ey, ain't no-bod-y ev-er gon-na love you the
w/ pick & fingers
let ring
C
Em
F
more than I, dear,
way I tried to, dear.
but I know that she
Who'll take all your
let ring
G
F6/G
C
Em
left you.
And you swear that you just don't know why.
pain, hon-ey, your heart ache, dear?
let ring

Am
Dm7
But you know, hon', I'll al - ways, I'll al - ways be a - round
And if you need me, you know that I'll al - ways be a - round
w/ pick & fingers
grad. cresc.
let ring
G
1.
2.
D.S. al Coda
if you ev - er want me. Come on and cry, cry,
if you ev - er want me. Come on and cry, cry,
Coda
Bridge
G
C
yeah.
And when you're walk - in' 'round the world, babe,
Gtr. 1
mf
F
G6
C
you said you try to look for the end of the road.
You might find out la - ter that the
Rhy. Fig. 1

F
G6
G7sus4
road will end in De - troit.
Hon - ey, the road don't e - ven end in Kat - man - du.
End Rhy. Fig. 1
let ring
10 9 8 8 8 9
10 10 10 8 10 10
12 12 8 8 10

Gtr. 1: w/ Rhy. Fig. 1, 3 1/2 times, simile
C
F
You could go all a - round the world
try'n' to find some-thin' to do with your

G6
G7sus4
C
life, babe.
Well, you on - ly got - ta do one thing well,

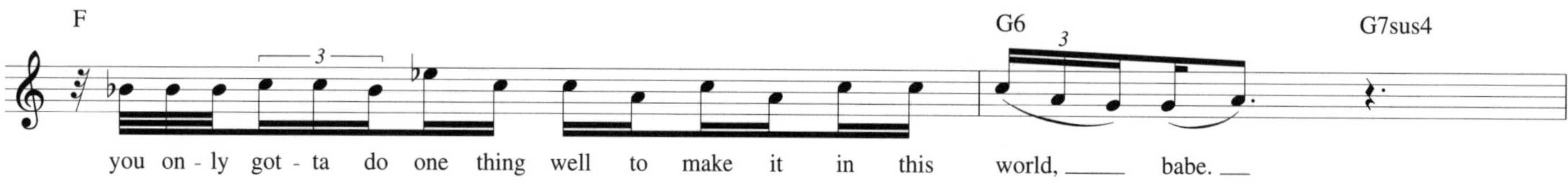
F
G6
G7sus4
you on - ly got - ta do one thing well to make it in this world, babe.

C
F
You got a wom - an wait - ing for you there, yeah.
All you ev - er got - ta do

G6
G7sus4
C
is be a good man one time to one wom-an, and that - 'll be the end of the road, babe.

D
G
I know you got more _ tears to shed, ___ babe.
So come on, ___ come on, ___ come on, _
Gtr. 1
grad. cresc.
let ring
Outro-Chorus
C
___ come on, ___ come on ___ and cry, cry, ___ ba - by. ___
f
F
C
F
___ Cry, ___ ba - by. ___ Cry. ___
w/ Voc. ad lib
C
F9
play 7 times
C
G
G♯m
Am
simile on repeats
2:3
rit.

from *Janis Joplin's Greatest Hits*

Down On Me

Words and Music by Janis Joplin

Verse
Gtr. 1: w/ Rhy. Fig. 3, 2 times
Gtr. 2 tacet
D C D C
1. One of these morn - ings be fine and fair.
2. Hard as gold, rain is rain.
lieve in your broth - er, (have) faith in man.
Gtr. 1: w/ Rhy. Fig. 2
D C D C D Cadd9
Hitch on my wings, babe, gon-na try out the air. And then it looks like ev-'ry - bod - y, in this whole
Had a gold - en man but he don't nev-er change, no. And it looks like ev-'ry - bod - y, in this whole
Help each oth - er, hon-ey, if you can. Be - cause it looks like ev-'ry - bod - y in this whole
Gtr. 2: w/ Fill 3, simile, 3rd time
G A D C
round world, yeah, (is) down on me,
round world, nah, nah, nah, (is) down on me.
round world, ev - 'ry - where I go, they're down on me,
Gtr. 1: w/ Rhy. Fig. 3
Gtr. 2: w/ Fill 1, 2nd time
Chorus
Gtr. 1: w/ Rhy. Fig. 1, 2 times
Gtr. 2: w/ Fill 2, 2nd & 3rd times, simile
D C D C D C
yeah. Hey, they're down on
You know they are, they're down on me,
oh, yeah, they're down on
Gtr. 2
full
let ring
Fill 1
Gtr. 2
Fill 2
Gtr. 2
let ring
full

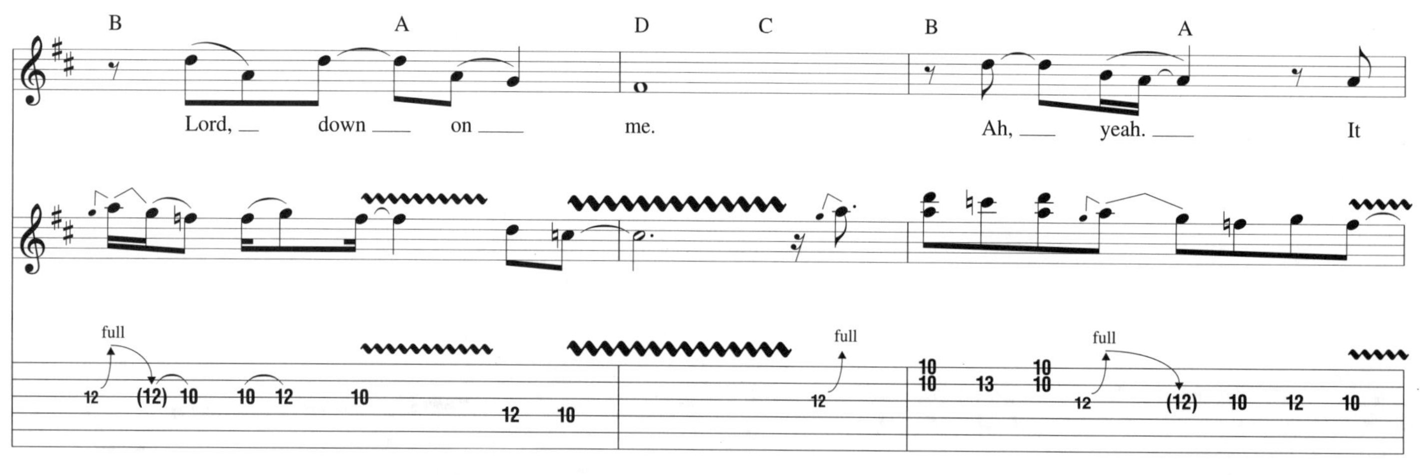
B
A
D
C
B
A
Lord, down on me.
Ah, yeah. It
full
full
full

To Coda 2
To Coda 1
Gtr. 1: w/ Rhy. Fig. 2
D
Cadd9
G
A
D
C
looks like ev - 'ry - bod - y, I said, in this whole round world, ah,

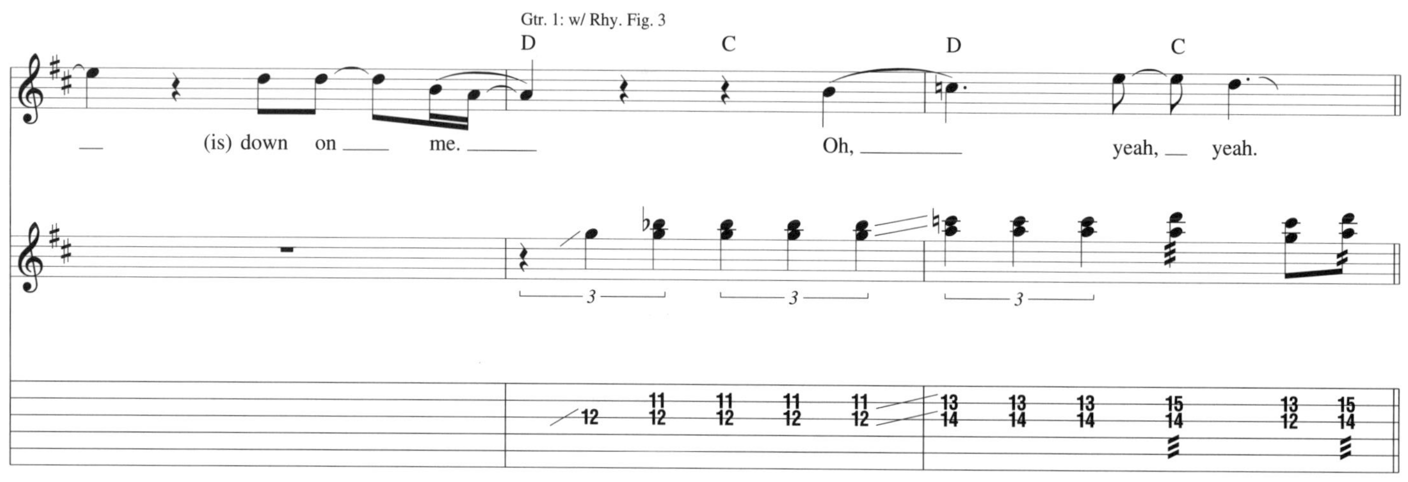
Gtr. 1: w/ Rhy. Fig. 3
D
C
D
C
(is) down on me. Oh, yeah, yeah.

Guitar Solo

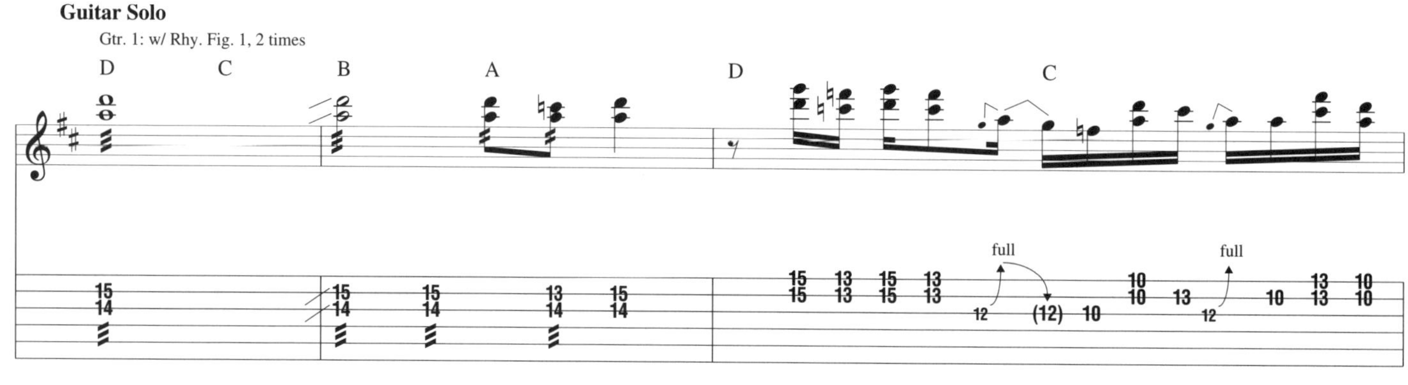
Gtr. 1: w/ Rhy. Fig. 1, 2 times
D
C
B
A
D
C
full
full

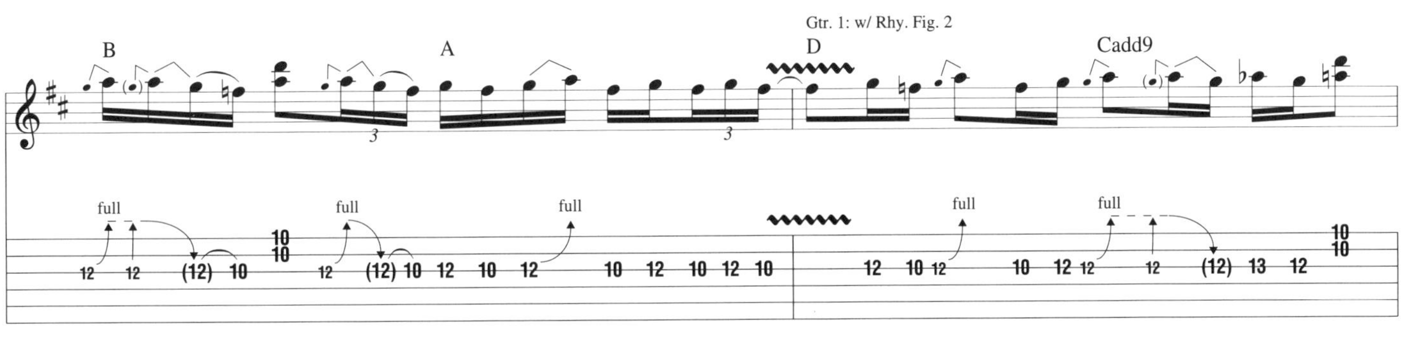
Gtr. 1: w/ Rhy. Fig. 2
B
A
D
Cadd9
full
full
full
full
full

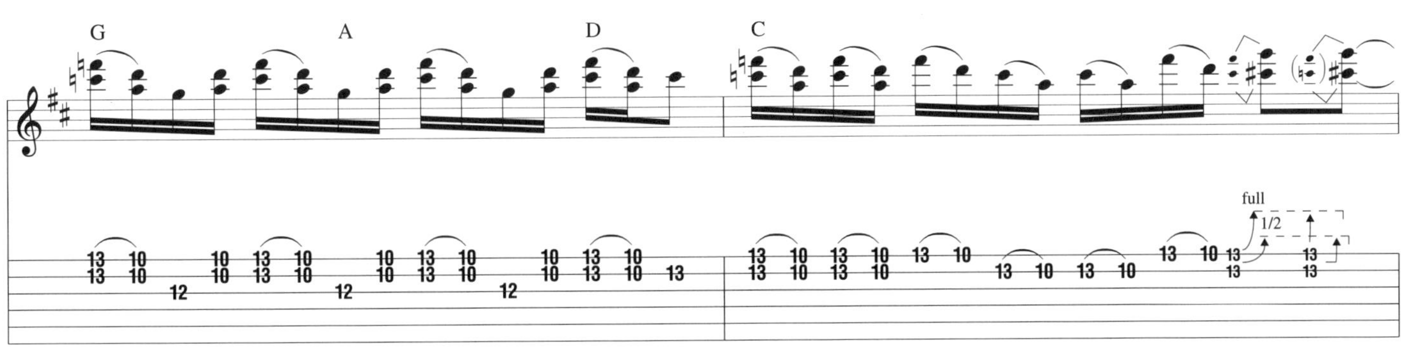
G
A
D
C
full
1/2

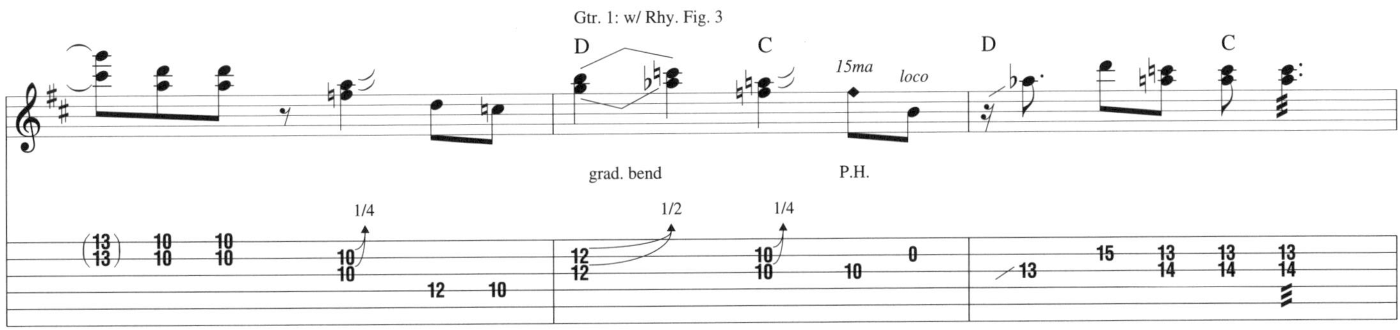
Gtr. 1: w/ Rhy. Fig. 3
D
C
15ma
loco
D
C
grad. bend
P.H.
1/4
1/2
1/4

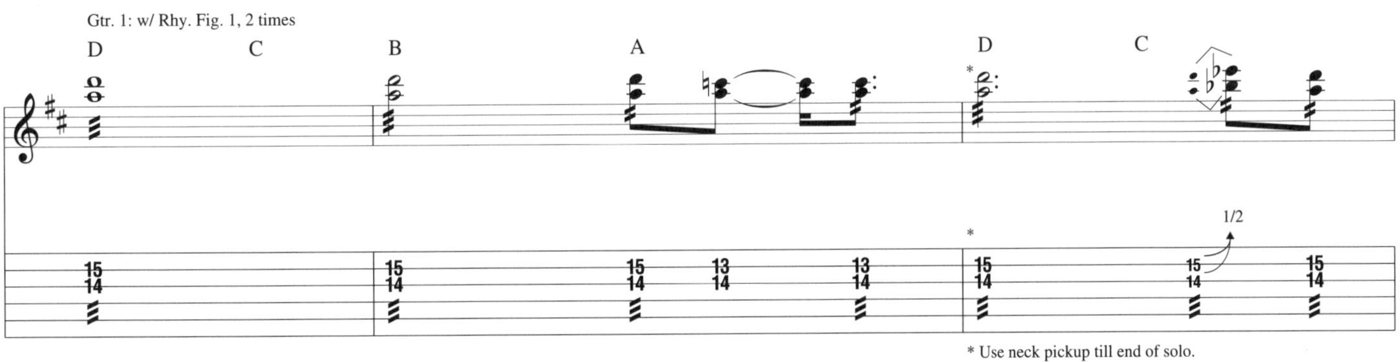
Gtr. 1: w/ Rhy. Fig. 1, 2 times
D
C
B
A
D
C
1/2
* Use neck pickup till end of solo.

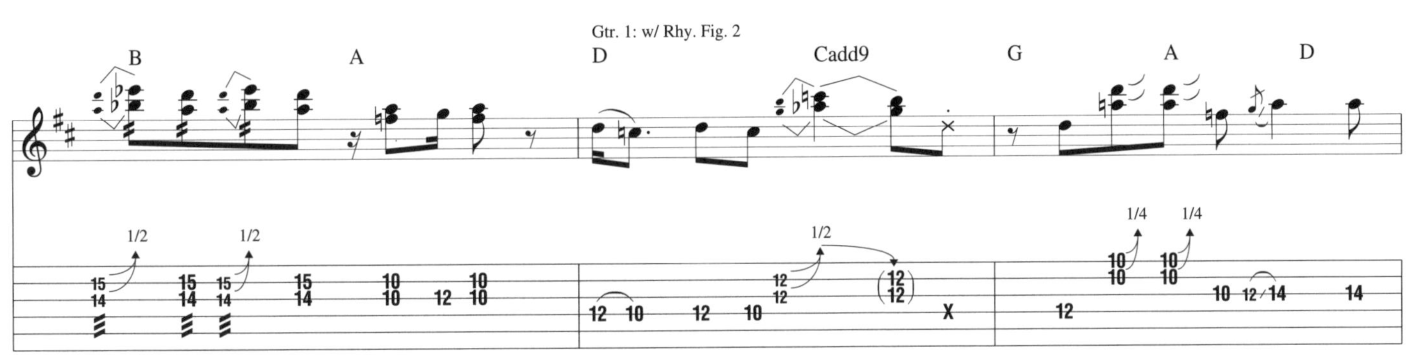
Gtr. 1: w/ Rhy. Fig. 2
B
A
D
Cadd9
G
A
D
1/2
1/2
1/2
1/4
1/4

D.S. al Coda 1

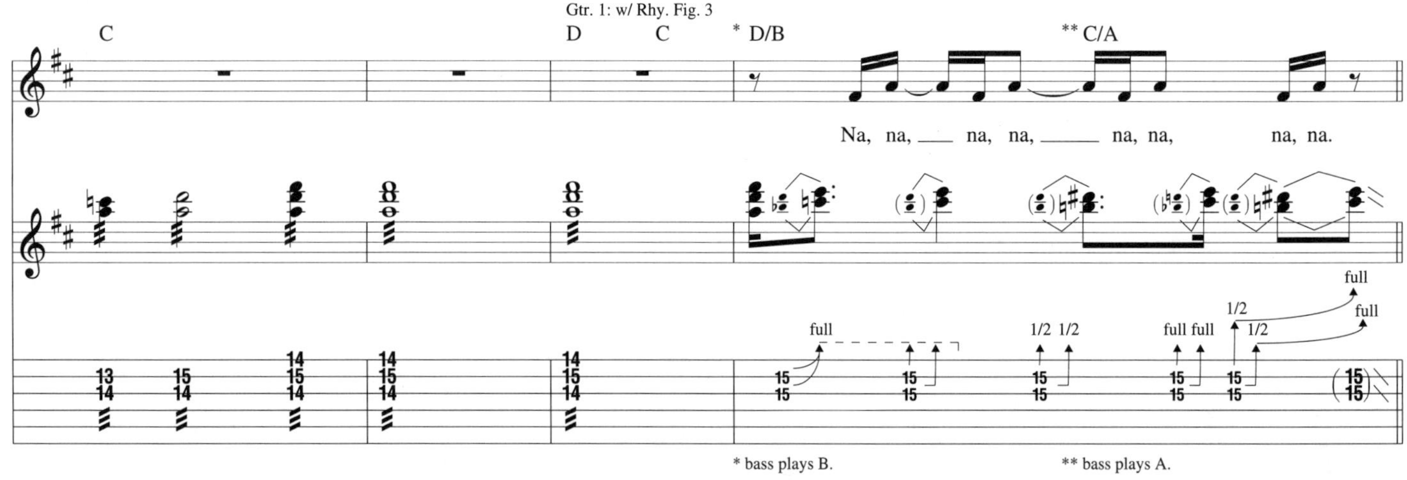
Gtr. 1: w/ Rhy. Fig. 3
C
D
C
* D/B
** C/A
Na, na, na, na, na, na, na, na.
full
1/2 1/2
full full
1/2
1/2
full
full
* bass plays B.
** bass plays A.

Coda 1
D.S. al Coda 2
Gtr. 1: w/ Rhy. Fig. 3
D
C
D
C
they're down on me, yeah.
Al - right, al - right.
3. Just be -
Fill 3
End Fill 3

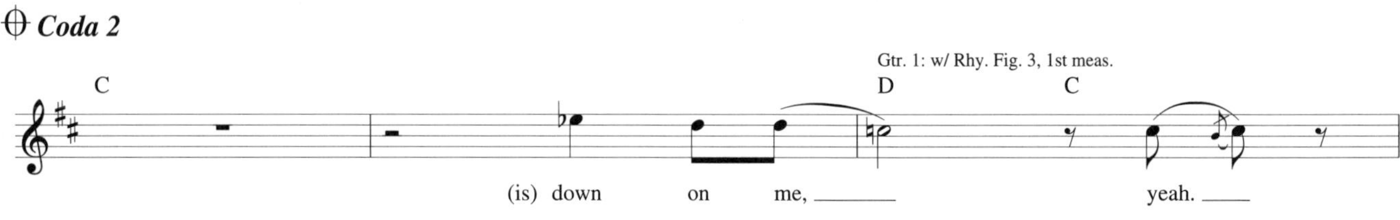
Coda 2
C
Gtr. 1: w/ Rhy. Fig. 3, 1st meas.
D
C
(is) down on me, yeah.

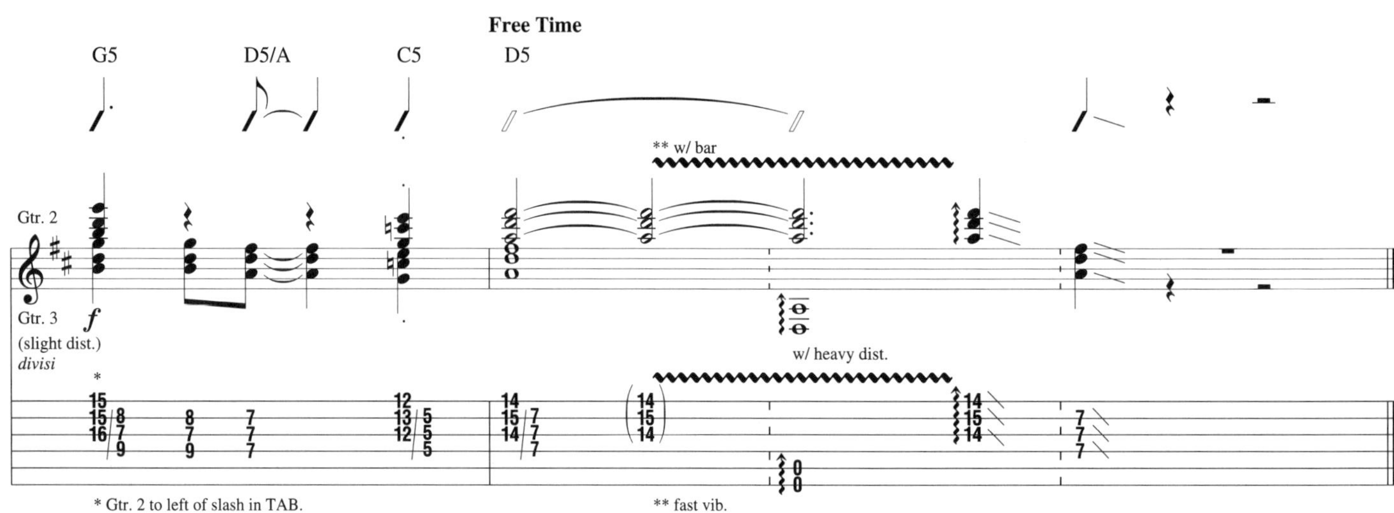
Free Time
G5
D5/A
C5
D5
** w/ bar
Gtr. 2
Gtr. 3
(slight dist.)
divisi
w/ heavy dist.
* Gtr. 2 to left of slash in TAB.
** fast vib.

from *Farewell Song*

Farewell Song

Words and Music by Sam Andrew

E5
F♯5
A
feel - ings, at all they've nev - er been heard. Well, I'm
known it. I guess I should have known it all a-long. Let me
E
A
D
C♯m
F♯m
talk - ing to you a - bout - a love. Did you hear me? I said love. Yeah, be-cause it's
hold you just once more. Oh, no, ask you just once more. Be-cause it's
4th time, To Coda
Bm
C♯m
Bm
C♯m
G
D/A
G
D/A
G
got to be such a long, long, long way from de - ny - ing, from de - ny - ing. And I say,
got to be such a long, long way from cry - ing, and I've been cry - ing. And I got
(Gtr. 1, cont. in slash, 2nd time)
1.
Gtr. 1: w/ Rhy. Fill 1
Gtr. 2: w/ Rhy. Fill 1A, simile, 2nd time
A
E5
F♯5
A
don't say no, no, no, no to me no more. 2. And I be -
Gtr. 2

2.
A
Asus2
A open
E5
F♯5
A
A
G♯
5fr
4fr
Gtr. 1
(cont. in notation)
tears in my eye. But don't you
Rhy. Fill 1A
End Rhy. Fill 1A
Gtr. 2
Bridge
F♯5
know when you love some-bod-y it's so pre-cious? And your beau-
(Woo, hoo.)
Rhy. Fig. 1
* Gtrs. 1 & 2 (slight dist.)
* composite arrangement
B5
C♯5
D5
E
F♯m
-ty could nev-er, nev-er, nev-er be had a-ver-y cheap-ly. No, no, no, no, no, no,
Gtr. 1
End Rhy. Fig. 1
full
Gtr. 2
End Rhy. Fig. 1

Guitar Solo
F#m7
N.C.
B5
C#5
D5
* C#5/E
no. __
full
full
* bass plays E
** B5/F#
F#m7
N.C.
F#m7
N.C.
1/4
1/2
1/2
1/2
Rhy. Fig. 1A
** bass plays F#.
B5
C#5
D5
E
F#m
You're gon - na have to pay
full
1/2
End Rhy. Fig. 1A
let ring

Bridge
Gtrs. 1 & 2: w/ Rhy. Figs. 1 & 1A, simile
F♯m7
your dues, and some-times, hon-ey, some-times you know you're bound to lose. Yeah, but
B5 C♯5 D5 E F♯5 G5 G♯5
Gtrs. 1 & 2: w/ Rhy. Fill 2
D.S. al Coda
(take repeat)
that's the way you're gon-na learn, learn, learn, to love deep - ly. 3. Yeah, oh, God, I
Coda
G D/A G D/A G
Outro
A A open
Gtr. 1
dy - ing, and I've been dy - ing. I say now... Ev-'ry day I got a lit-tle bit babe. I say now,
Gtr. 2
(Gtr. 1, cont. in slash)
Double-Time Feel
E5 F♯5 A E5 F♯5 A
Rhy. Fig. 2
End Rhy. Fig. 2
ev-'ry day I lose me. Set foot in my heart. I've been lone - ly, lone-ly. Look a-round, peo - ple, see now.
Riff A
End Riff A
Rhy. Fill 2
Gtrs. 1 & 2

Gtr. 1: w/ Rhy. Fig. 2, 3 times, simile
Gtr. 2: w/ Riff A, 3 times, simile
E5
F♯5
A
I've got - ta find, I've got - ta want, I've got - ta need. Here goes - a.

E5
accel.
F♯5
A
He's my ba - by, ba - by. Talk a - bout my ba - by.

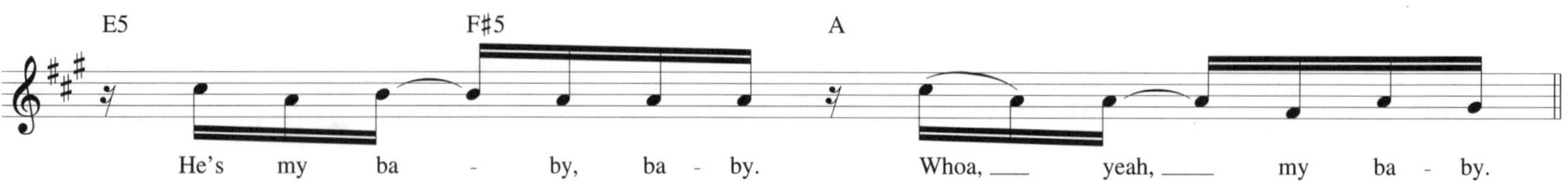
E5
F♯5
A
He's my ba - by, ba - by. Whoa, yeah, my ba - by.

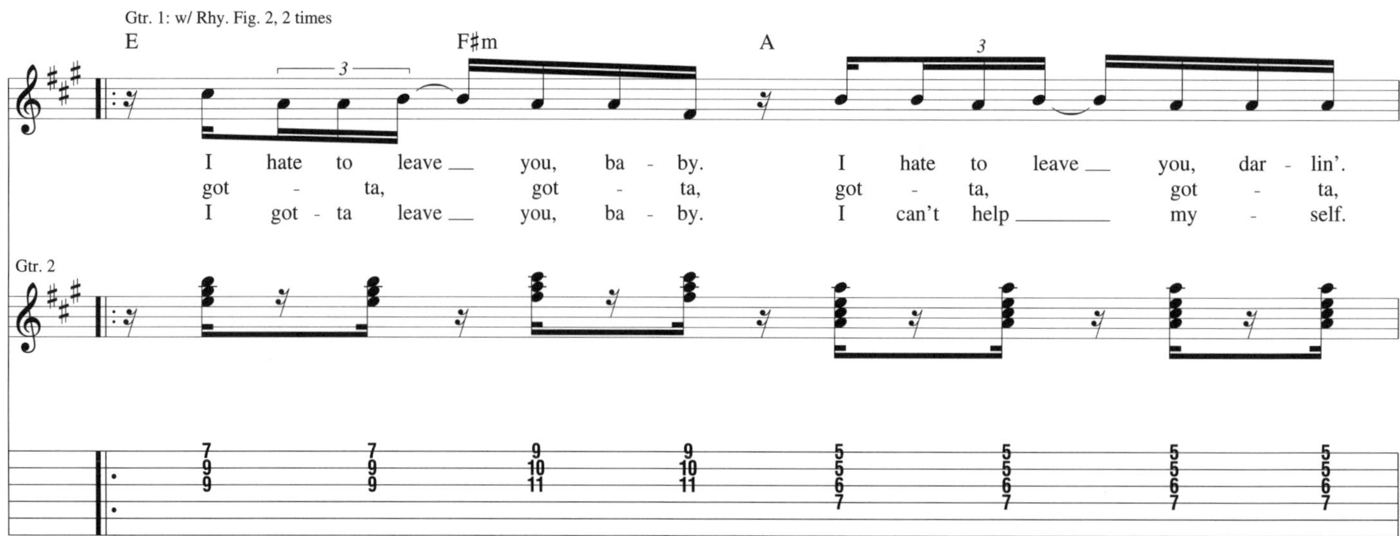
Gtr. 1: w/ Rhy. Fig. 2, 2 times
E
F♯m
A
I hate to leave you, ba - by. I hate to leave you, dar - lin'.
got - ta, got - ta, got - ta, got - ta,
I got - ta leave you, ba - by. I can't help my - self.
Gtr. 2

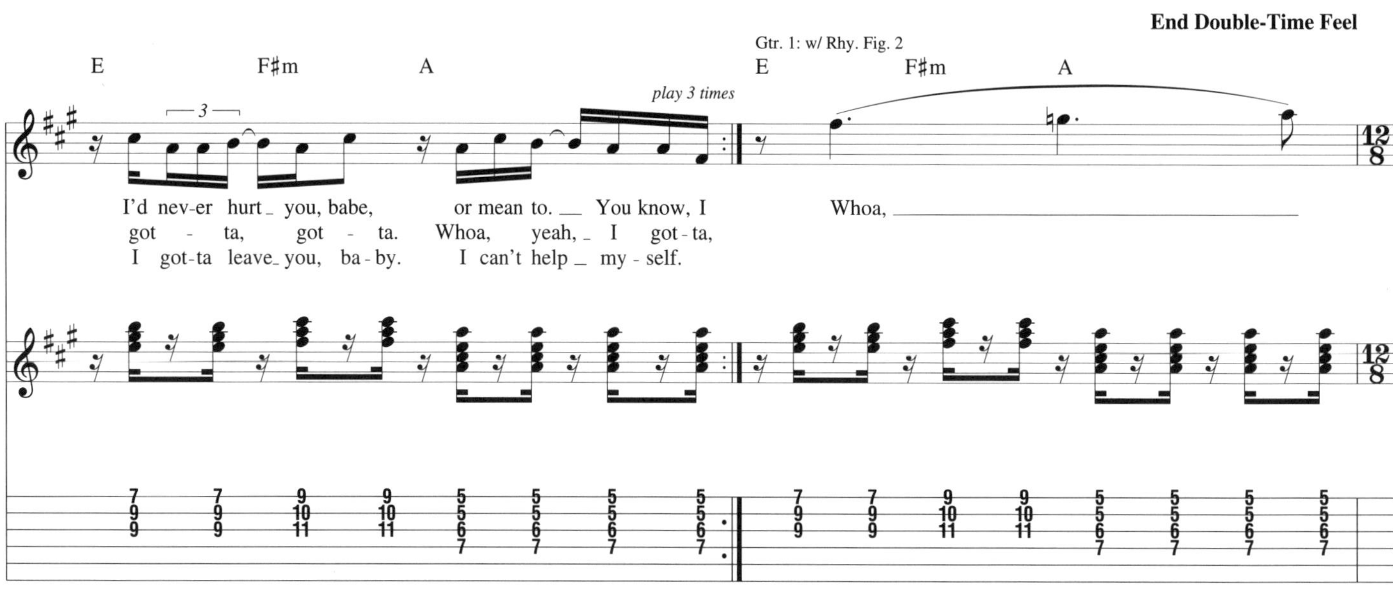
End Double-Time Feel
Gtr. 1: w/ Rhy. Fig. 2
E
F♯m
A
play 3 times
I'd nev-er hurt you, babe, or mean to. You know, I
got - ta, got - ta. Whoa, yeah, I got-ta,
I got-ta leave you, ba-by. I can't help my-self.
Whoa,

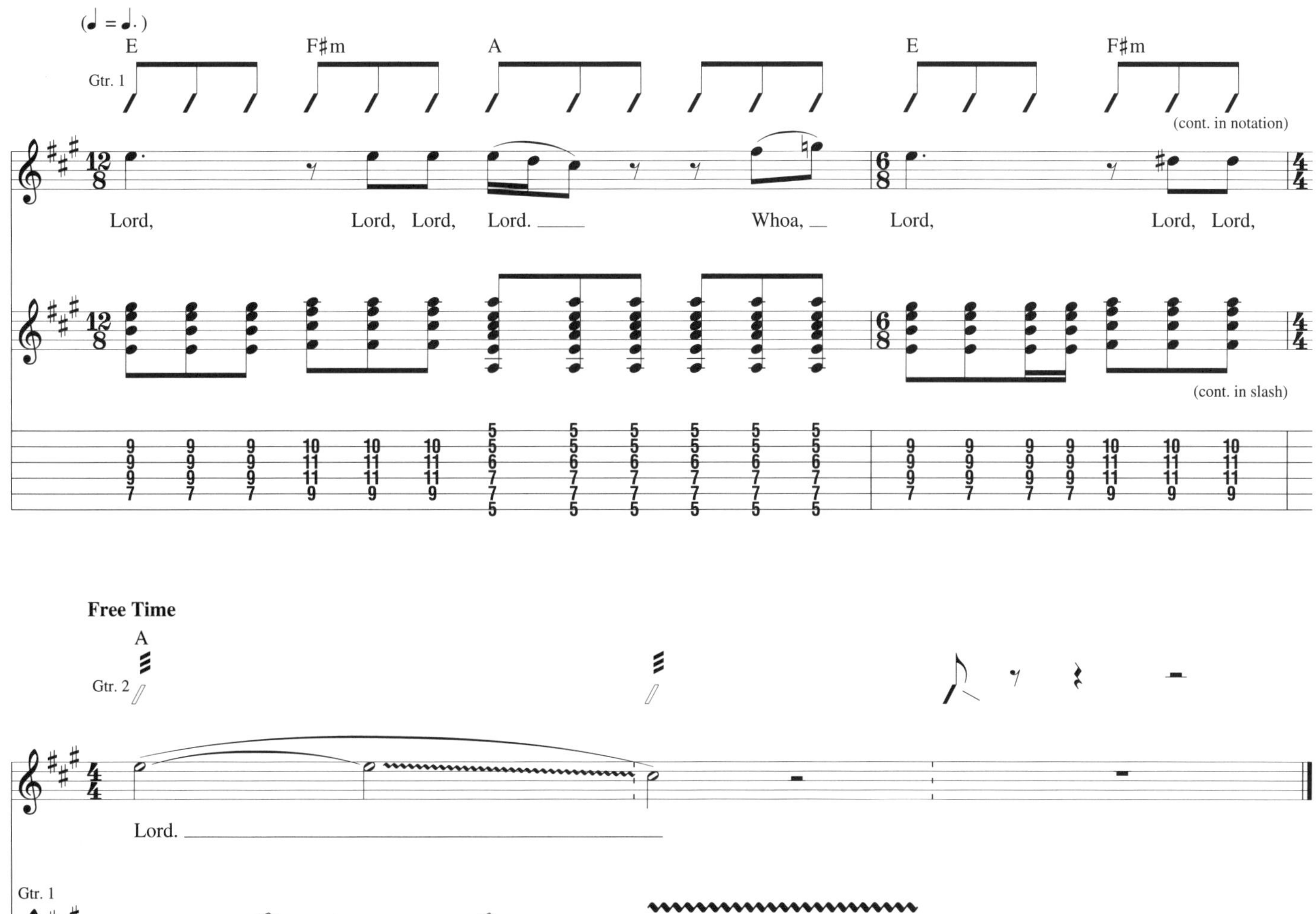

Additional Lyrics

3. Yeah, oh, God, I wish I could explain to myself,
'Cause I know that it's my fault too.
It's so easy to hurt you darlin'.
It's so hard, I guess it's hard not to do.
And I know that you showed me a new life,
And you'll always, yeah, you'll always be my friend.
Babe, but I don't think that I can keep from trying,
And I've been trying.
And I've been trying for you, babe. Yes, I have now.

4. Well, tell me, tell me, tell me, tell me, tell me.
What would I do without you, child? I'm afraid I can't say.
But I hope, honey, that I would, would remember.
But, Lord, it would be, it would be such a sunny day.
No, no, no, now good-bye, and I'll see you sometime.
And don't be weary; everything's just fine.
Babe, but I don't think that I can keep from dying,
And I've been dying.
I say now…

from *Pearl*

Get It While You Can

Words and Music by Jerry Ragovoy and Mort Shuman

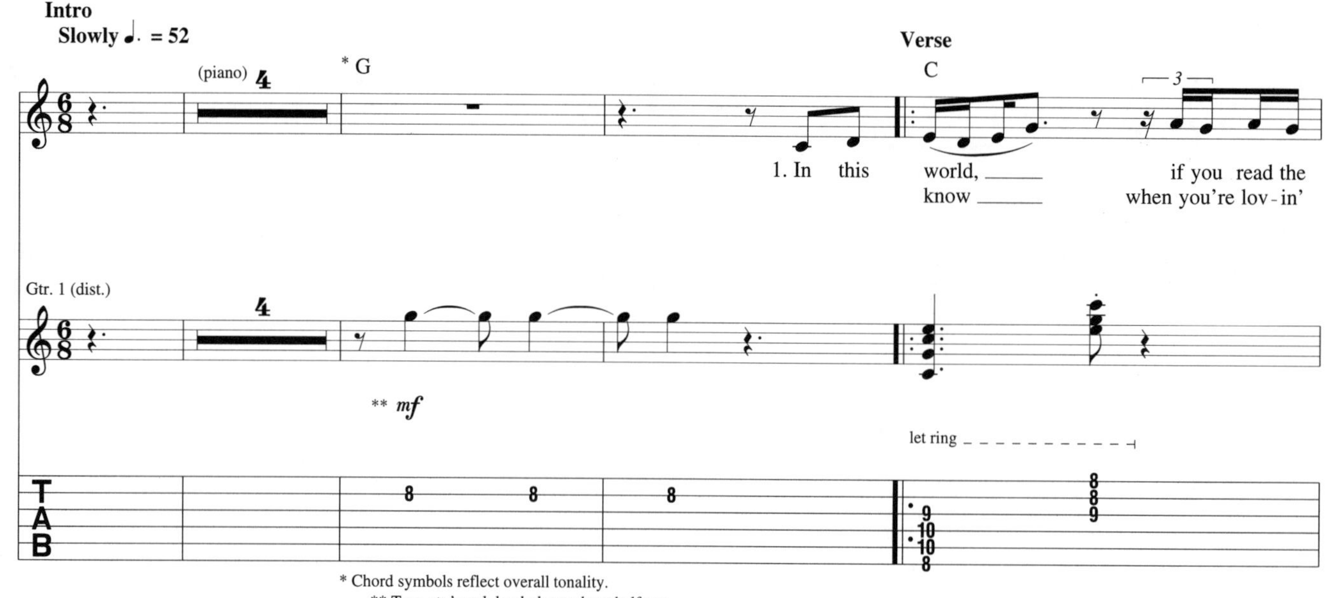

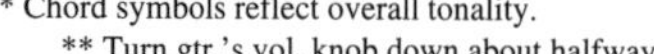

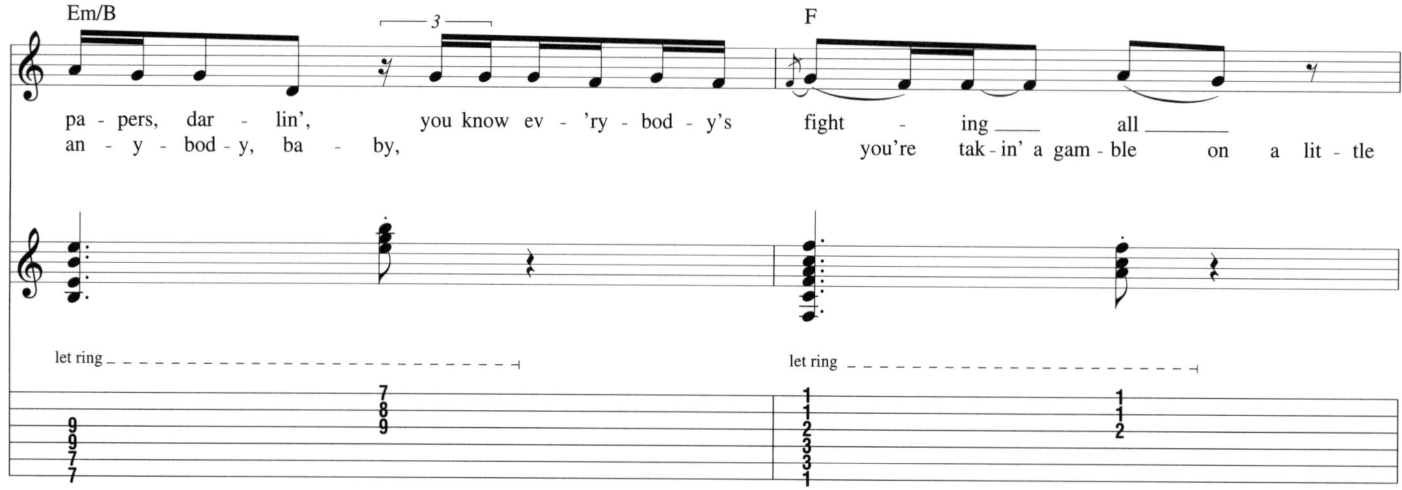

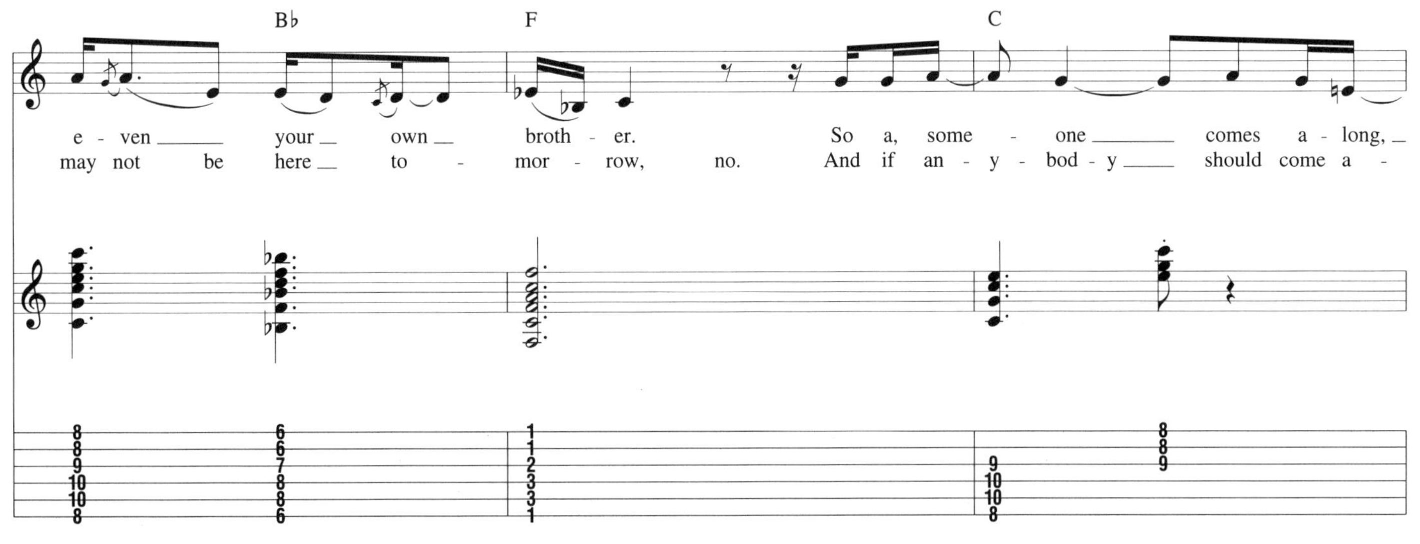

* On D.S., reduce gtr's vol. as before.

B♭ F C G
1. Hey, hey, get it while you can. Don't you turn your back on
2., 3. Hey, hey, get it while you can. Don't you turn your back on
yeah, yeah.
To Coda
1.
2.
Am G G
love. No, no. 2. Don't you no. No, no, no, no,
love. No, no,
*f
* Turn gtr.'s vol. knob up to 10.
Guitar Solo
C Em/B F
no.
full
C B♭ C E7
8va
rake
1/2
full

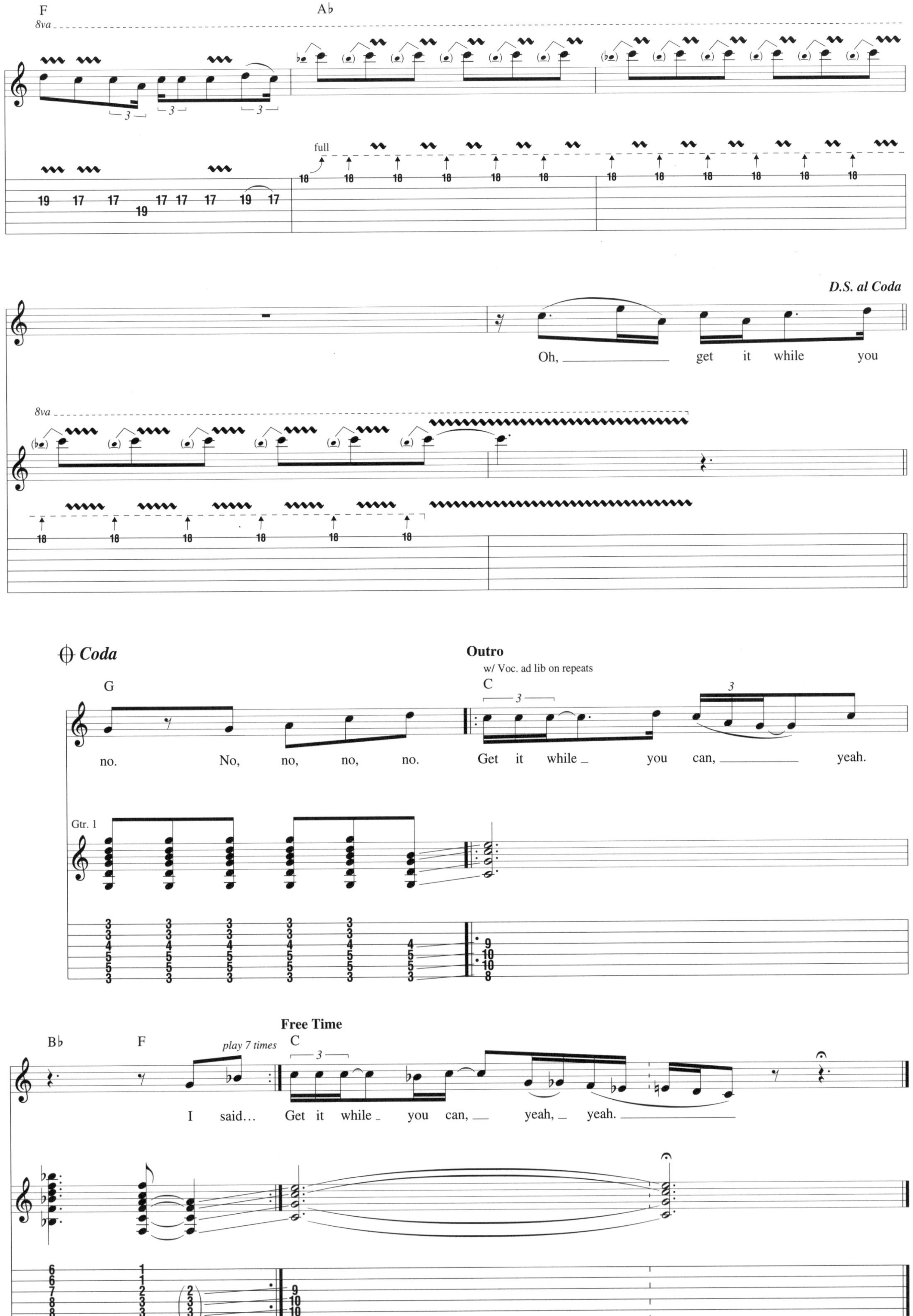
F
8va
Ab
full
D.S. al Coda
Oh, get it while you
Coda
Outro
w/ Voc. ad lib on repeats
G
C
no. No, no, no, no. Get it while you can, yeah.
Gtr. 1
Bb
F
play 7 times
Free Time
C
I said… Get it while you can, yeah, yeah.

from *Cheap Thrills*

I Need a Man to Love

Words and Music by Janis Joplin and Sam Andrew

Intro

Moderately Slow Rock ♩ = 96

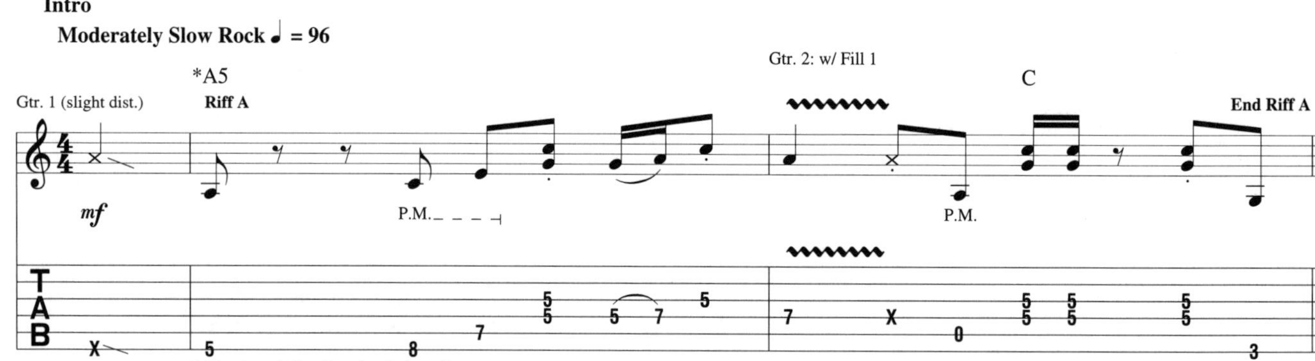

* Chord symbols reflect implied tonality.

Guitar Solo

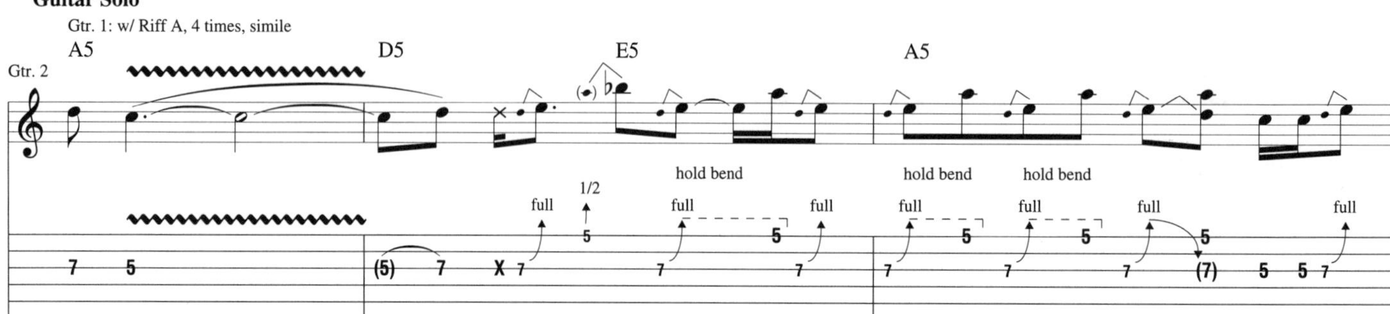

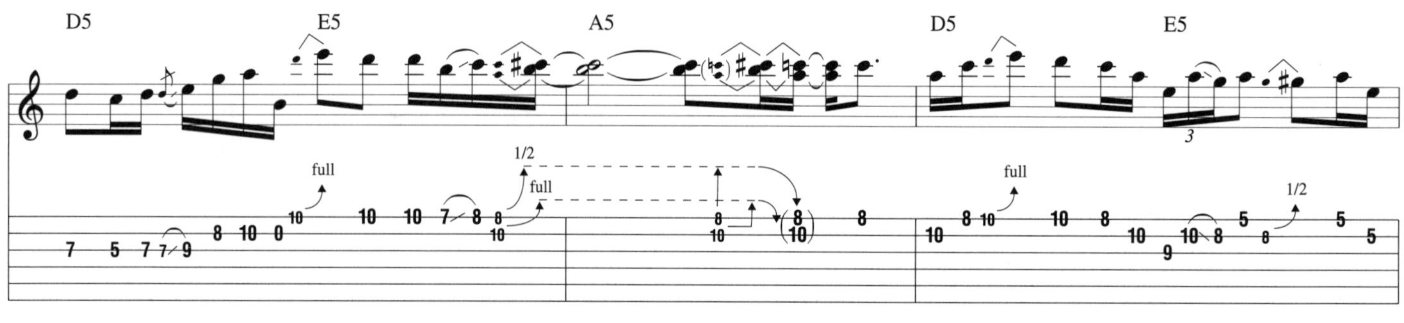

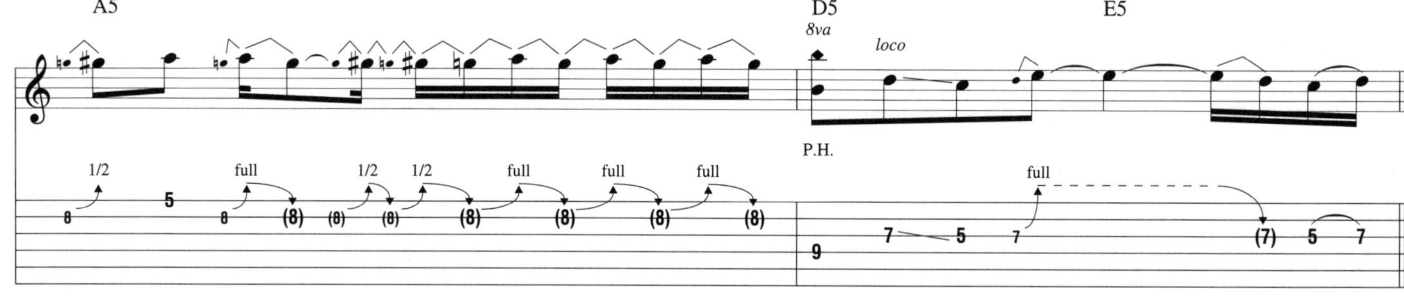

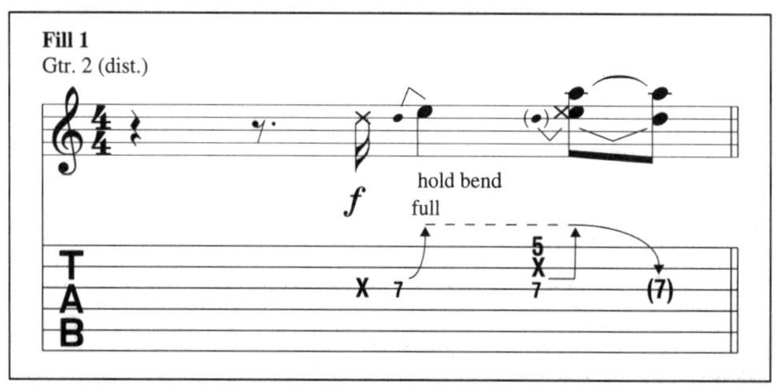

Verse
Gtr. 1: w/ Riff A, 4 times, simile
Gtr. 2 tacet
A5
D5
E5
1. Oh, I, I need a man to love me.
2. Whoa, won't you let me hold you?
3. Oh, I, I need a man to love me.
Don't you un - der - stand me, ba - by,
Hon - ey, just close your eyes.
Oh, may - be you can help me, please,
why
Whoa,
why
I need a man to love?
won't you let me hold you, dear?
I need a man to love?
I wan - na just...
But I be-lieve that...
Gtr. 2
simile on repeats
full
Pre-Chorus
F♯m
G
B
A5/B
N.C.
1. I got - ta find him, I got - ta have him like the air I breathe. I want a
2., 3. See Additional Lyrics
(Whoa, whoa, whoa.
* Gtrs. 1 & 2
* composite arrangement

F♯m G B A5/B B A5/B N.C.
lov - in' man to un - der - stand. Can't be too much for me. You know it
Whoa, whoa, whoa,
F♯ G G♯ A A♯ B
can't be now, can't be now, can't be now, can't be now, can't be now. Can't be this
Oh, no. Oh, no. Oh, no. Oh, no. Oh, no.
Chorus
Gtr. 1: w/ Riff A, 4 times, simile
Gtr. 2 tacet
D E A5
lone - li - ness, ba - by, sur - round ing me. No, no, no, it just can't be.
Oh.)
Bkgd. Voc.: w/ Voc. Fig. 1, 4 times, 1st & 2nd times
Bkgd. Voc.: w/ Voc. Fig. 1, 3 times, 3rd time
D5 E5 A5 D5 E5
1. There's got to be some kind of an - swer.
2. Oh, ba - by, ba - by, ba-by, just can't be, no, no, no.
3. Oh, ba - by, ba - by, ba-by, ba - by, just can't be.
Voc. Fig. 1
(No, it just can't be.)

A5
D5
E5
And ev - 'ry - where I look there's ___ none a - round. ___
And why did - n't an - y - one ev - er tell ___ me now?
And who could be fool - in' me? ___
To Coda
A5
D5
E5
1.
A
6
5fr
Gr. 1
P.M.
Whoa, ___ it can't be. ___
I wake _ up one morn-ing and I re - al - ize. ___
I got all ___
Oo, whoa, _ whoa, _ yeah,

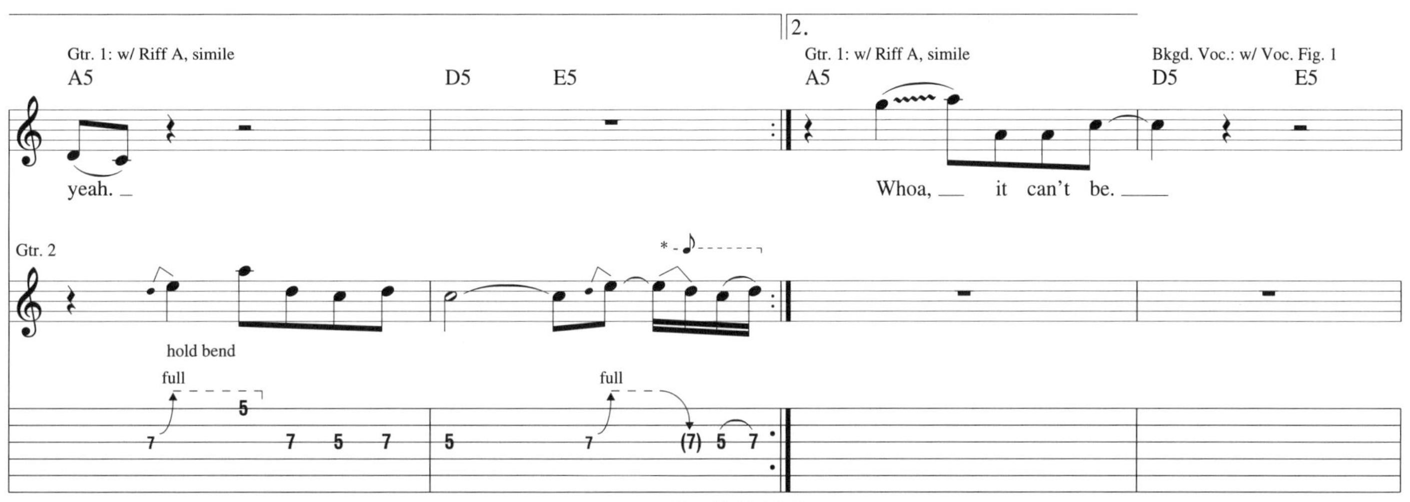

Gtr. 1: w/ Riff A, simile
A5
D5
E5
2.
Gtr. 1: w/ Riff A, simile
A5
Bkgd. Voc.: w/ Voc. Fig. 1
D5
E5
yeah. _
Whoa, ___ it can't be. ___
Gtr. 2
hold bend
full
full

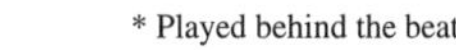

* Played behind the beat.

Guitar Solo
Gtr. 1: w/ Riff A, 7 times, simile
Gtr. 2: w/ Riff B, 7 times, simile
A5
A5
D5
E5
A5
I'm gone.
Gtr. 3
Gtr. 3 (slight dist.)
Gtr. 1
divisi
w/ amp tremolo
full
1/2
grad. release
P.M.
let ring

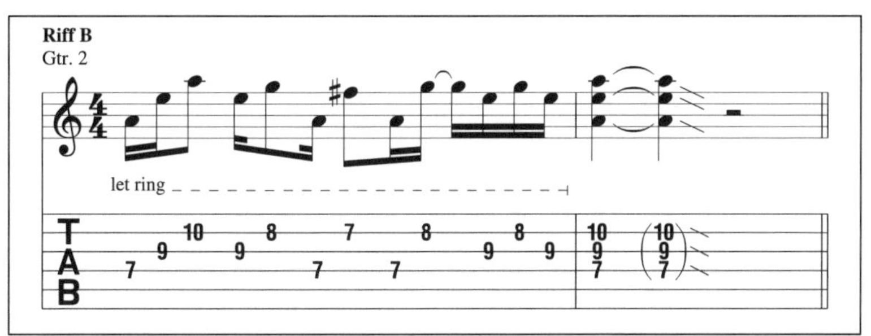

Riff B
Gtr. 2
let ring

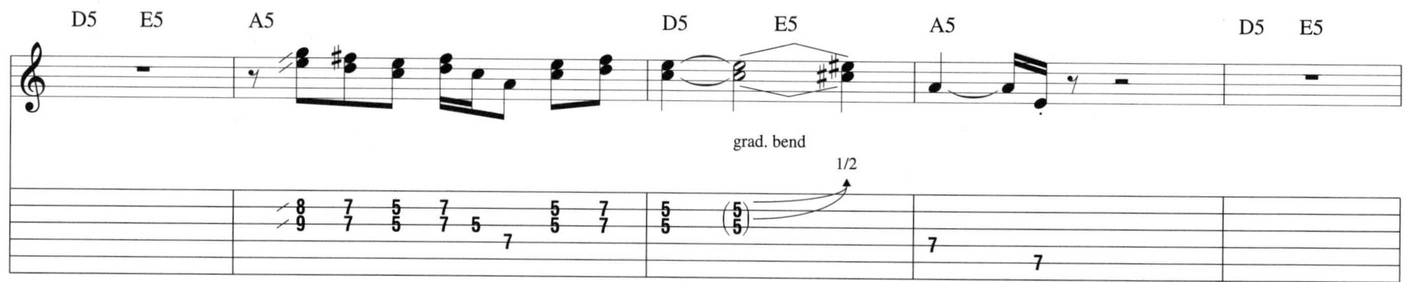

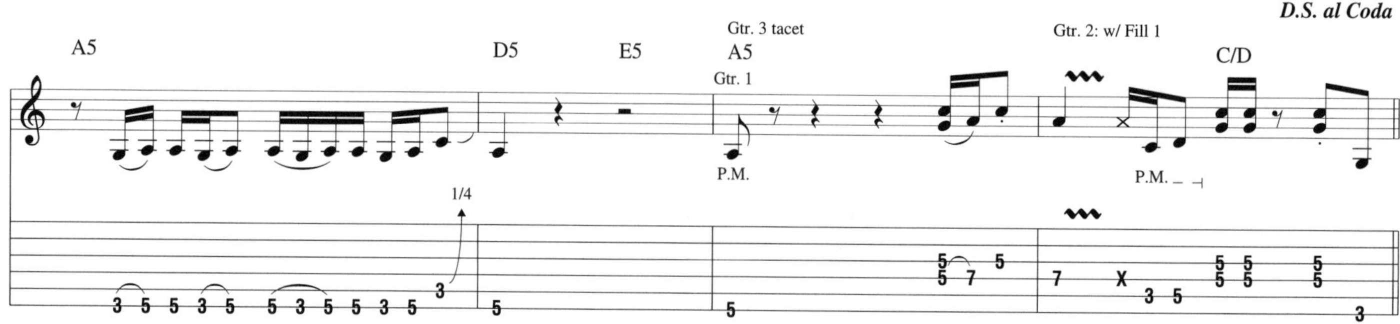

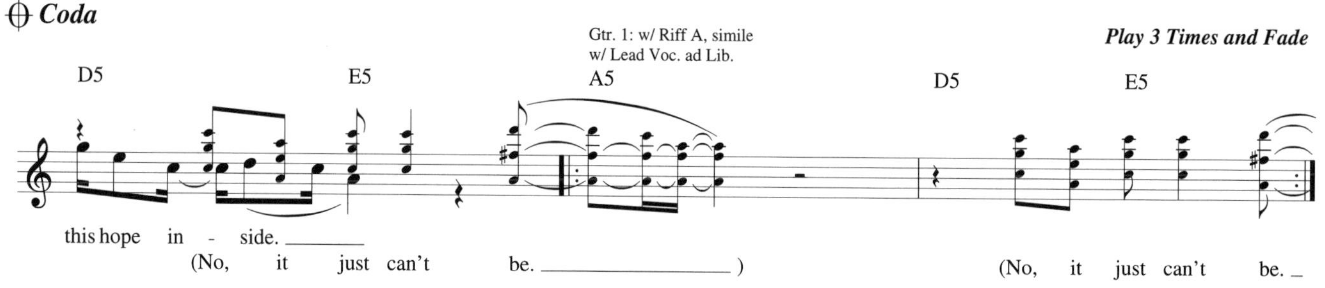

Additional Lyrics

2. I wanna just put my arms around you
   Like the circles are goin' around the sun.
   And let me hold you, daddy,
   At least until the morning comes.
   Because it can't be now, can't be now,
   Can't be now, can't be now, can't be now.
   Can't be this loneliness,
   Baby, surrounding me.

3. But I believe that someday and somehow,
   Said, it's bound to come along.
   Because when all my dreams and my plans
   Just cannot turn out wrong.
   You know it can't be now, can't be now,
   Can't be now, can't be now, can't be now.
   Can't be this loneliness,
   Baby, surrounding me.

from *I Got Dem Ol' Kozmic Blues Again Mama!*

Kozmic Blues

Words and Music by Janis Joplin and Gabriel Mekler

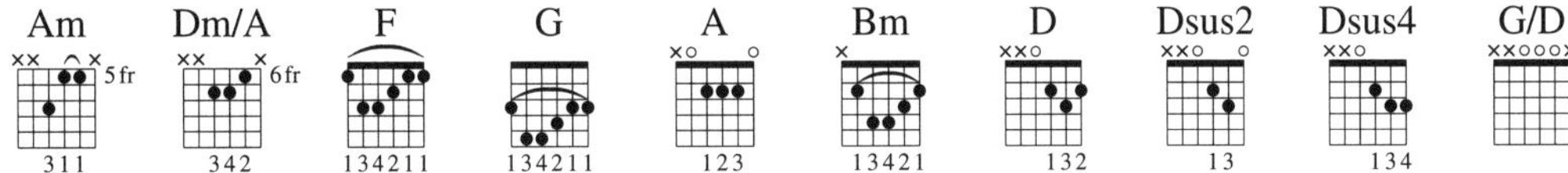

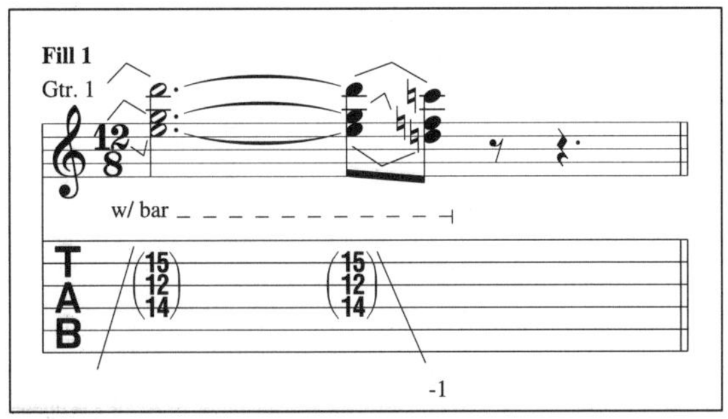

Am
Am/G
Am/F♯
F
friends, they turn a - way.
Twen-ty five years, hon-ey, just-a one night. Oh, yeah.
Well, I know that they don't come with age, no, no.
Gtr. 1
Gtr. 2
divisi
w/o slide
(Gtr. 2, cont. in slash)
To Coda
F
G
F
G
Gtr. 2
(cont. in notation)
I keep mov-ing on but I nev-er find out why. I keep
Well, I'm twen-ty five years old-er now, so I know it can't be right. And I'm no
I ain't nev-er gon-na love you an-y bet-ter, babe, and they're nev-er gon-na love you right, so you'd bet-ter
Gtr. 1
Am7
1.
E7
push-in' so hard and, babe, I keep try'n to make it right to an - oth-er lone-ly day. Oo, whoa,
bet-ter, babe, and I can't help you no more than I did when
Rhy. Fill 1
End Rhy. Fill 1
Gtr. 1
Rhy. Fill 1A
End Rhy. Fill 1A
Gtr. 2
let ring

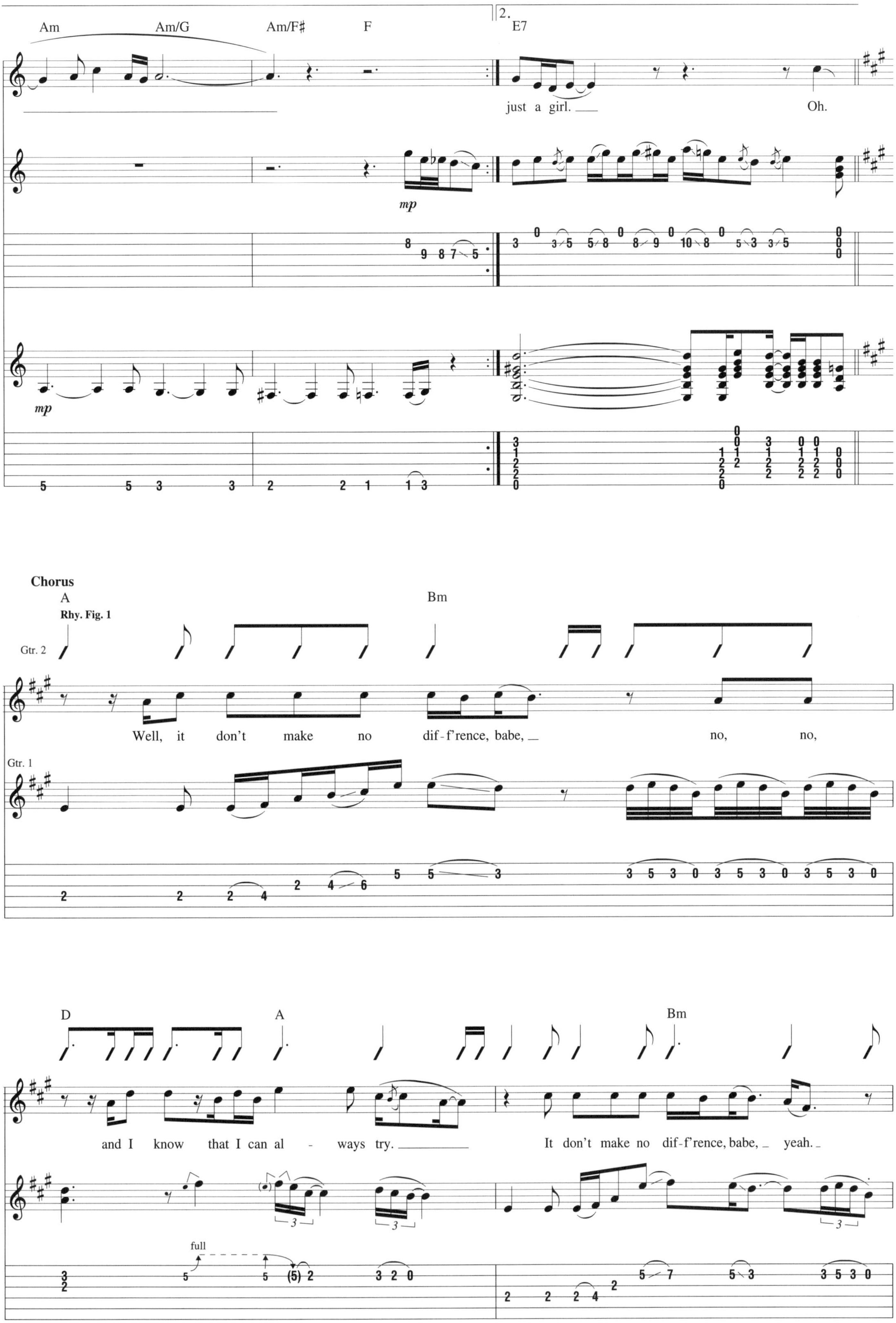

Am Am/G Am/F♯ F

2. E7

just a girl. Oh.

mp

mp

Chorus

A Bm

Rhy. Fig. 1

Gtr. 2

Well, it don't make no dif-f'rence, babe, no, no,

Gtr. 1

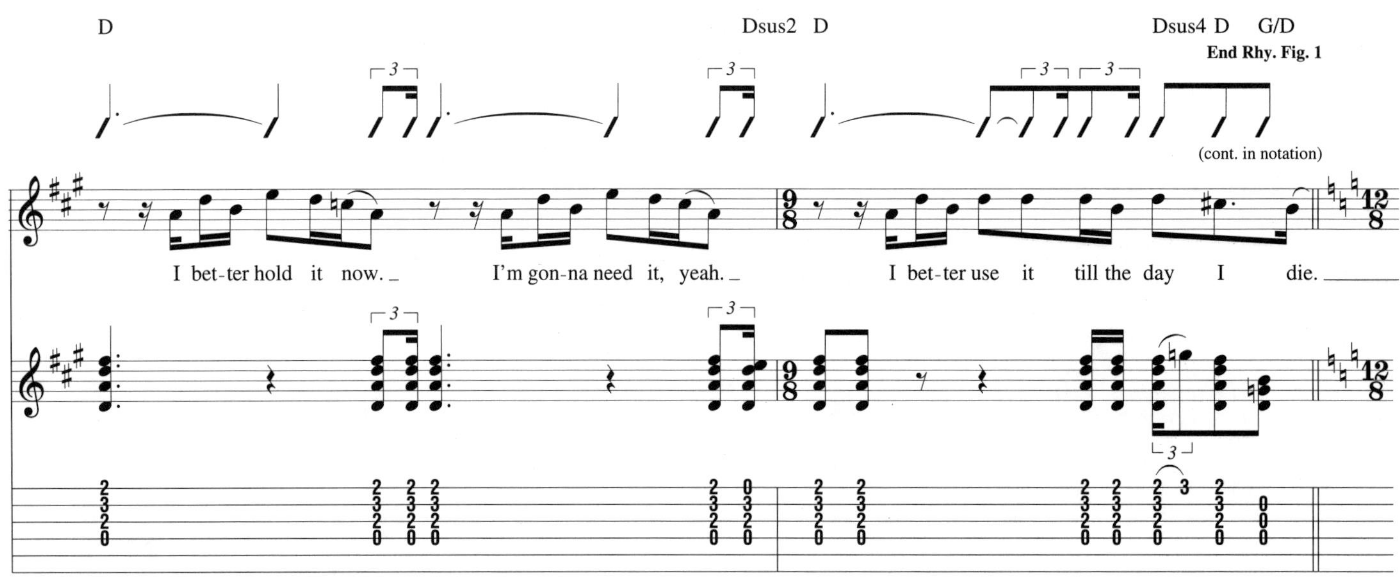

D
Dsus2 D
Dsus4 D G/D
End Rhy. Fig. 1
(cont. in notation)
I bet-ter hold it now.
I'm gon-na need it, yeah.
I bet-ter use it till the day I die.

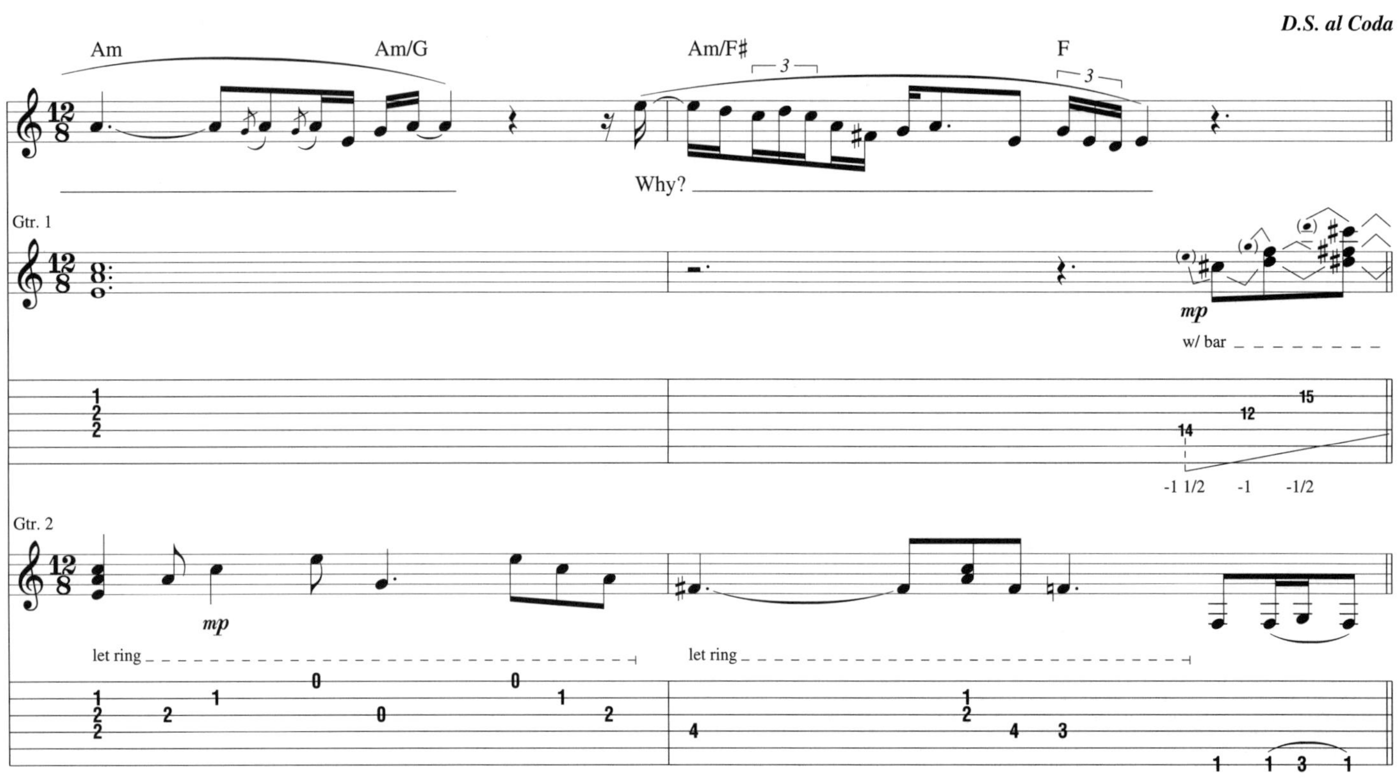

D.S. al Coda
Am
Am/G
Am/F♯
F
Why?
Gtr. 1
mp
w/ bar
Gtr. 2
mp
let ring
let ring

Coda
Chorus
Gtrs. 1 & 2: w/ Rhy. Fills 1 & 1A, simile
Gtr. 2: w/ Rhy. Fig. 1, 1 4/5 times, simile
Am7
A
Bm
dig it now, right now. Oh!
Well, it don't make no dif-f'rence, babe,
Gtr. 1

D
A
Bm
and I know that I can al - ways try.
Well, there's a fire in-side of ev-'ry one of us.
w/ pick & fingers

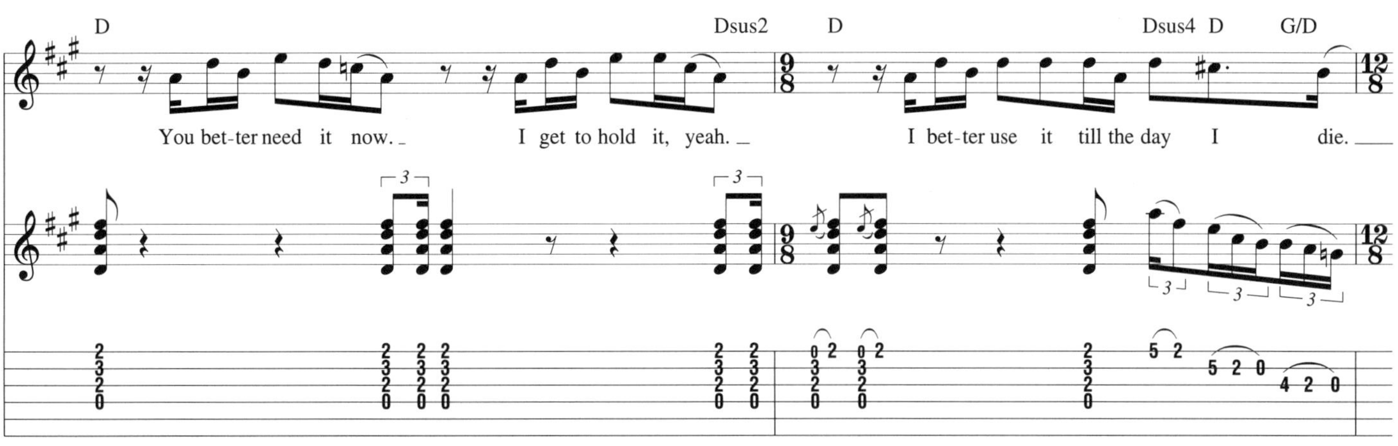
D
Dsus2
D
Dsus4
G/D
You bet-ter need it now.
I get to hold it, yeah.
I bet-ter use it till the day I die.

A
Bm
D
A
Don't make no dif-f'rence, babe, no, no, no,
and it nev - er, ev - er will,
hey.
let ring

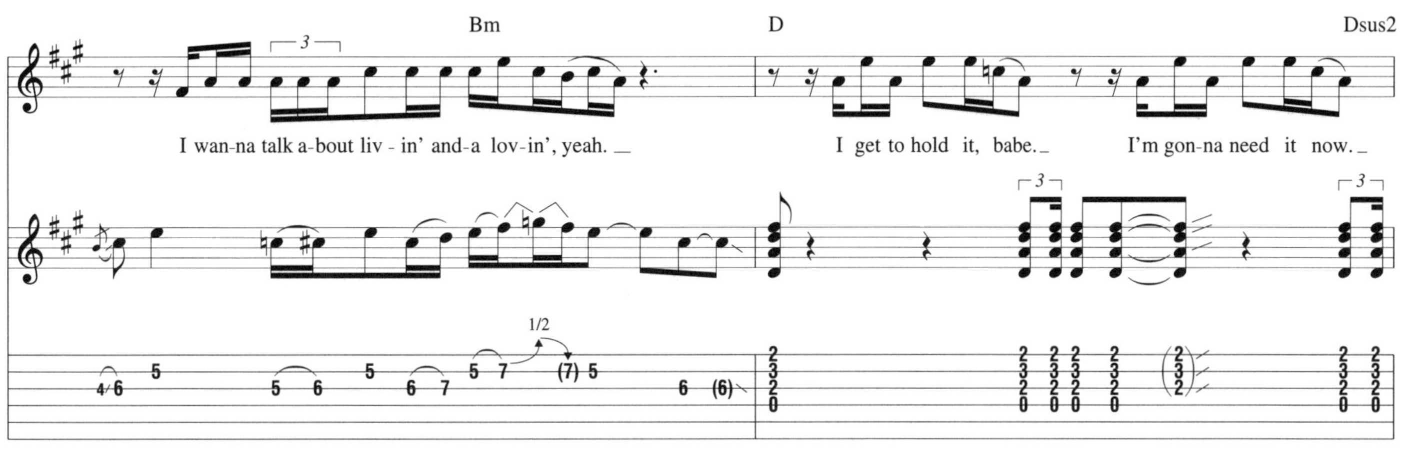
Bm
D
Dsus2
I wan-na talk a-bout liv - in' and-a lov-in', yeah.
I get to hold it, babe.
I'm gon-na need it now.
1/2

Outro
Gtr. 2: w/ Rhy. Fill 2
Gtr. 2: w/ Rhy. Fig. 1, 1st 2 meas., simile, till fade
D
A
A
Bm
I bet-ter use it. Say, oh.
Don't make no dif-f'rence, babe.
w/ bar
D
A
Oh hon-ey, I hate to be the one.
I said, you bet - ter
let ring
Bm
D
A
live your life, and you bet-ter love your life.
Oh be - lieve, some-day you're gon-na have to cry.
Yes, in-deed.
full
1/2
1/2
hold bend
w/ pick & fingers
Bm
D
A
Yes, in - deed.
Yes, in - deed.
Oh ba - by, yes, in - deed.
I said, you,
w/ pick & fingers
Rhy. Fill 2
Gtr. 2

Bm
they're al - ways gon - na hurt you.
I said, they're al - ways gon - na let you down,
full
1/2
D
A
I said, ev-'ry-where, ev-'ry-day.
Ev - 'ry-day
and ev - 'ry-way,
ev - 'ry-way.
w/ pick & fingers
1/4
Oh hon-ey, won't you hold on, see what's gon - na move.
I said, it's
let ring
gon - na dis - ap - pear when you turn your back.
I said, you know it ain't gon - na be there when you

Begin Fade

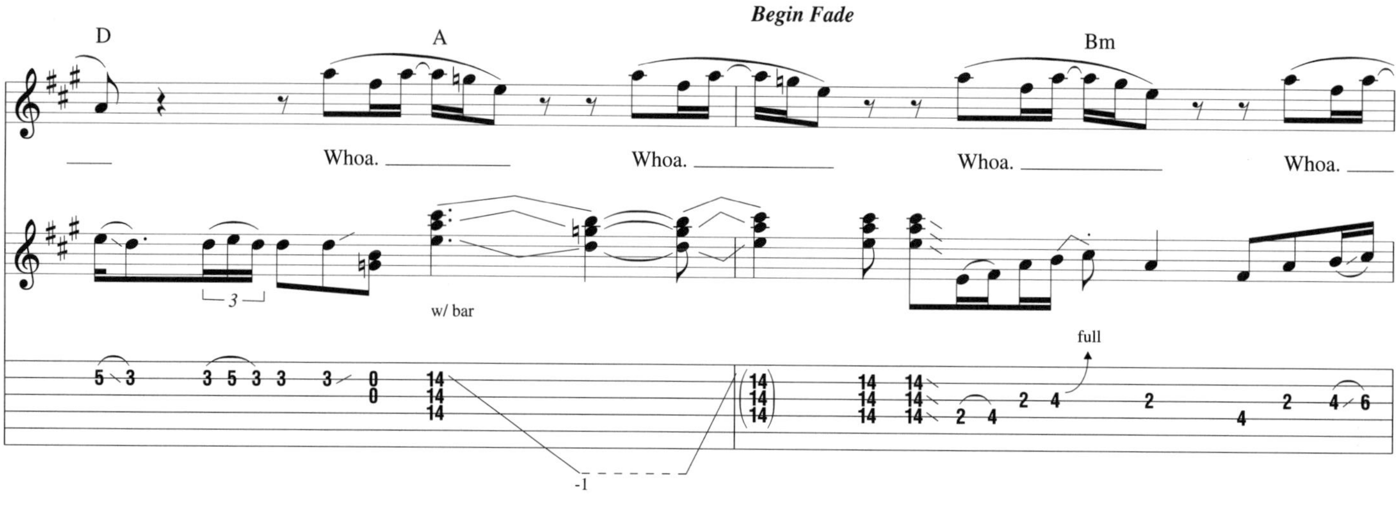

Fade Out

from *I Got Dem Ol' Kozmic Blues Again Mama!*

Little Girl Blue

Words by Lorenz Hart
Music by Richard Rodgers

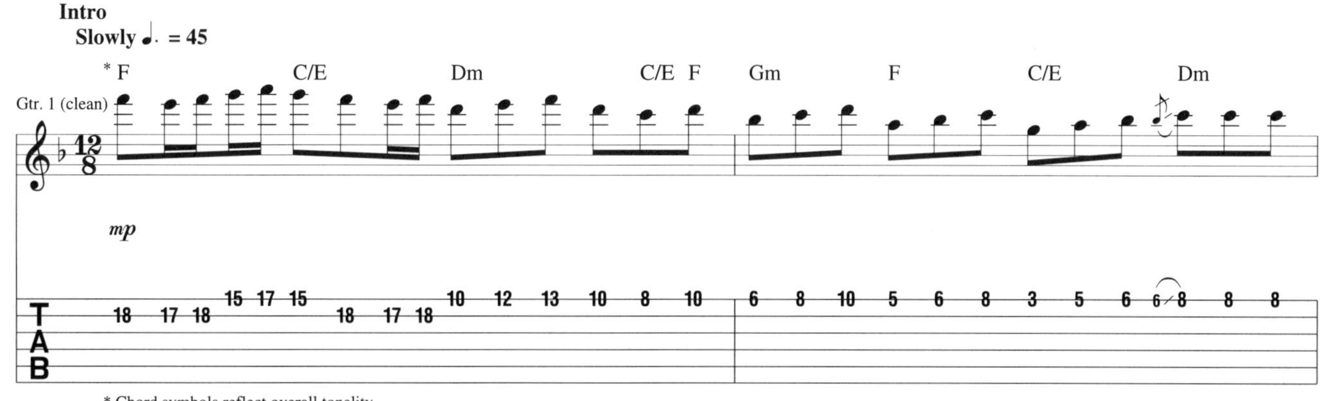

* Chord symbols reflect overall tonality.

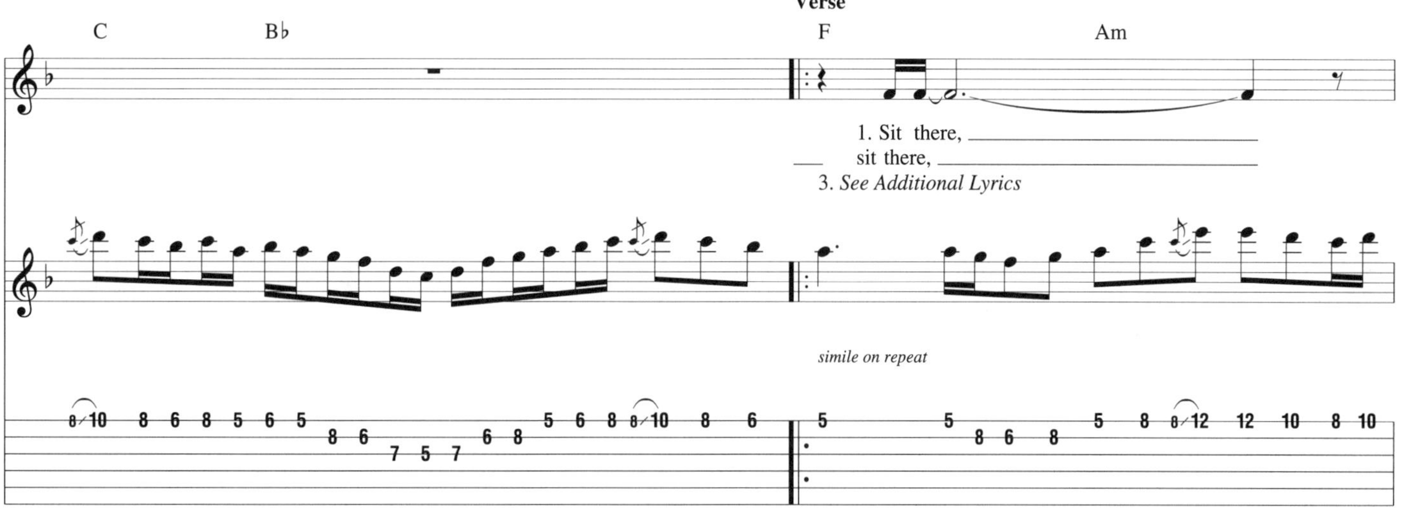

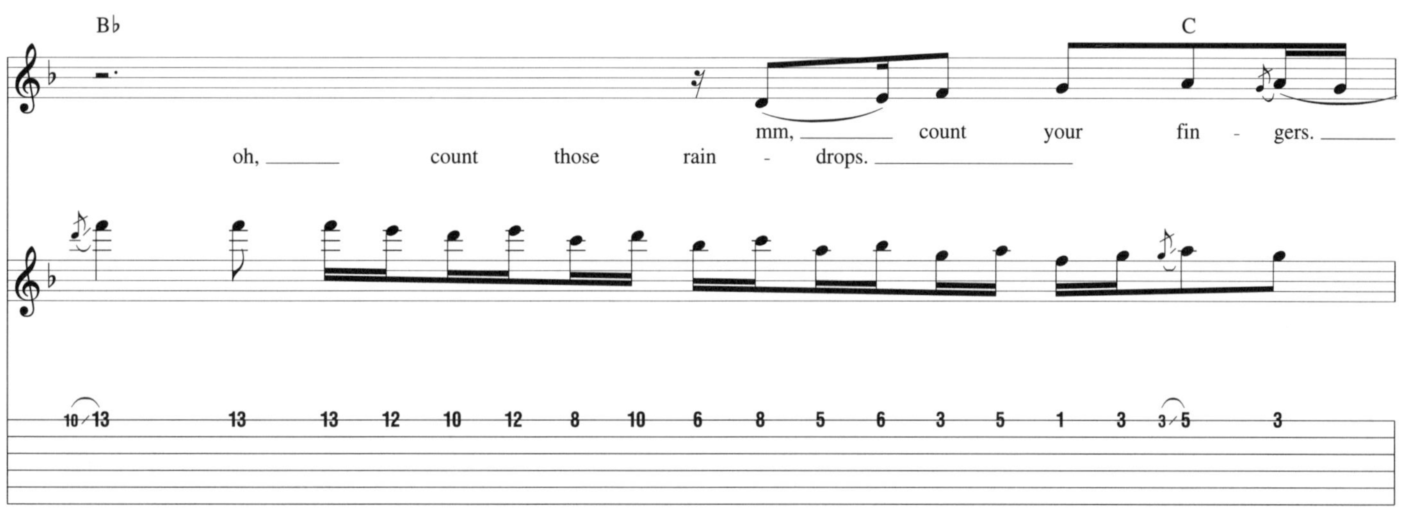

F
Fmaj7
What else,
what else is there
Oh, feel 'em fall - in' down,
oh
hon - ey, all a -
F7
to do?
Oh
round you.
Hon - ey, don't you
mf
B♭
Am
hon - ey, I know how you feel.
I know you feel
that
know it's time?
I feel it's time
some - bod - y told you,
mp
Gm
you're through,
oh,
while I,
'cause you got to know
that all
you ev - er gon - na have to count

F
Am/E
I sit there. Mm,
on or gon-na wan-na lean on. It's gon-na feel
B♭/D
Am/D
Gm/C
F/C
count, oh, count your lit-tle fin-gers my un-hap-
just like those rain-drops do when they're fall-
B♭
1., 2.
F
-py, oh, lit-tle girl, lit-tle girl blue, yeah.
in' down, hon-ey, all a-round you.
C/E
Dm
C/E F
Gm
F
C/E
Dm
Oo, I know you're un-hap-py.

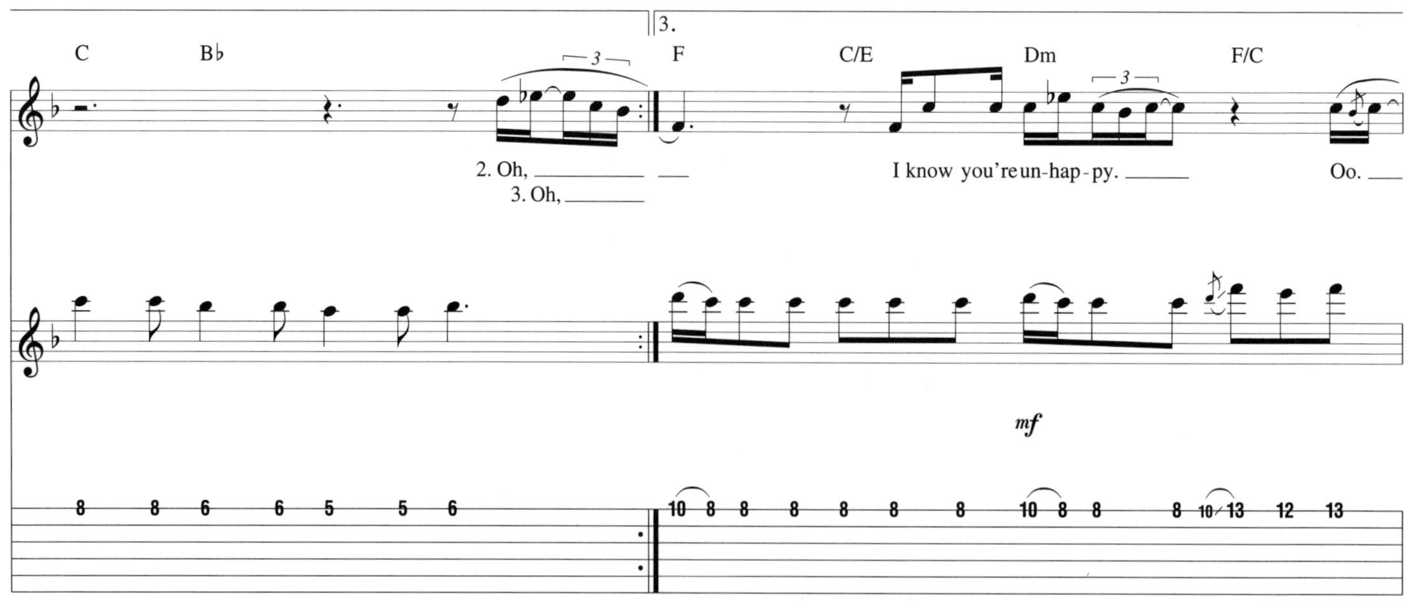

Additional Lyrics

3. Oo, sit there
   Oh, go on, go on and count your fingers.
   I know what else, what else
   Hon' have you got to do.
   And I know how you feel,
   And I know you ain't got no reason to go on.
   And I know you feel that you must be through.
   Oh, honey go on and sit right back down.
   I want you to count
   Oo, count your fingers.
   Oh, my unhappy, my unlucky,
   And my little old girl blue.
   I know you're unhappy.
   Oo, oh hon' I know,
   Baby, I know just how you feel.

from *I Got Dem Ol' Kozmic Blues Again Mama!*

Maybe

Words and Music by Richard Barrett

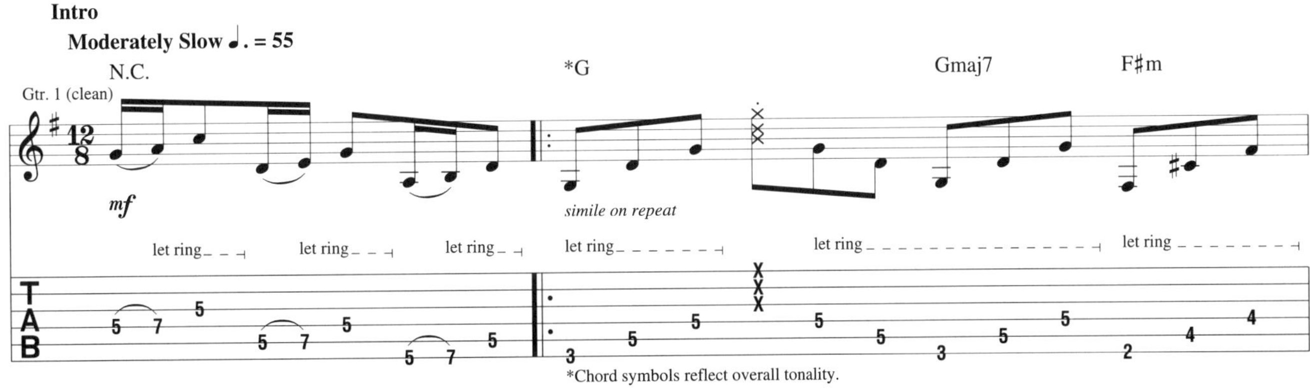

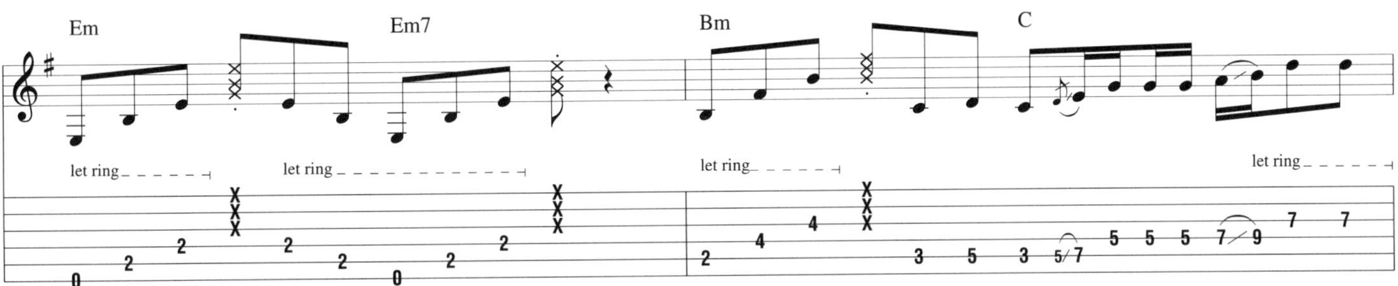

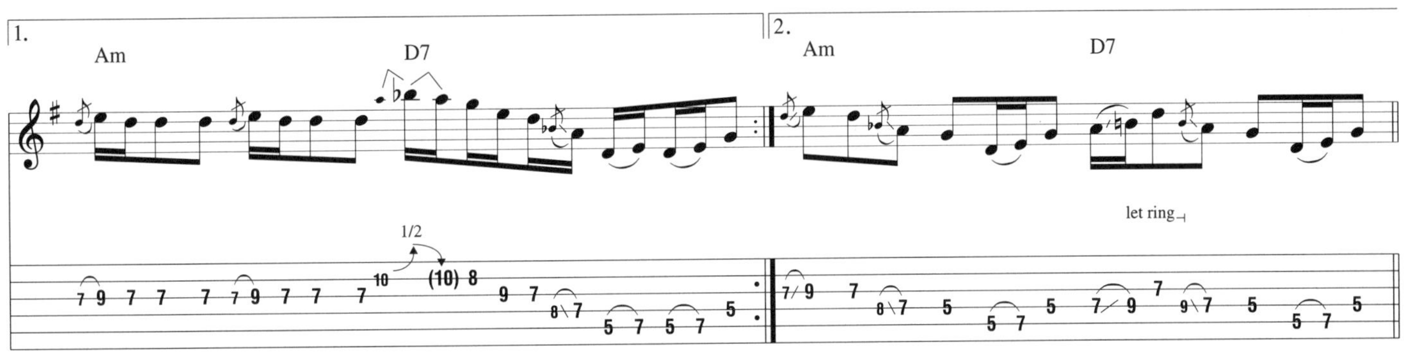

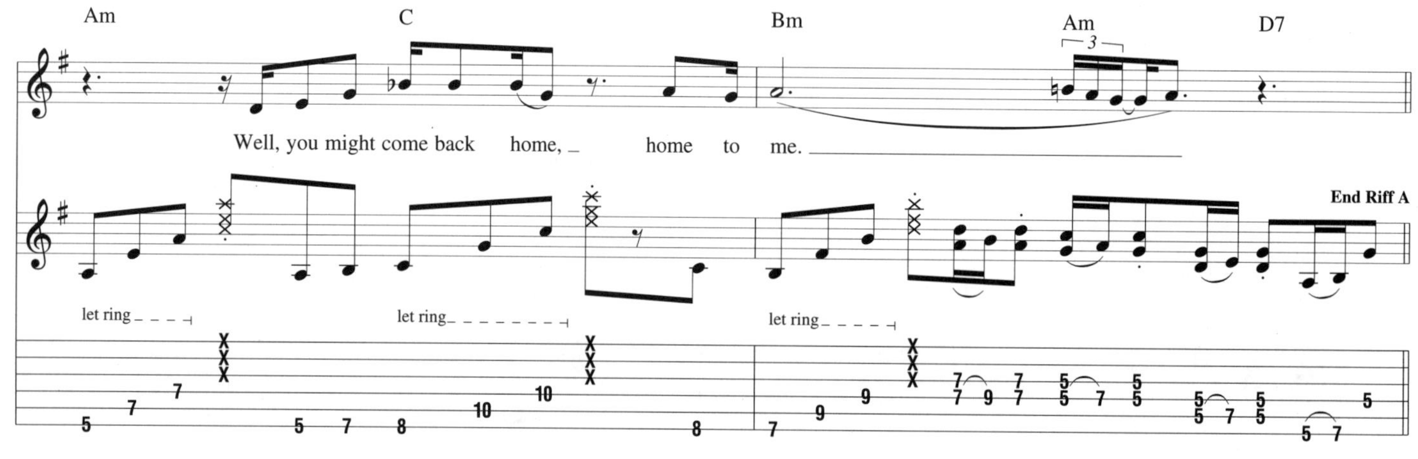
Am
C
Bm
Am
D7
Well, you might come back home, home to me.
End Riff A
let ring
let ring
let ring

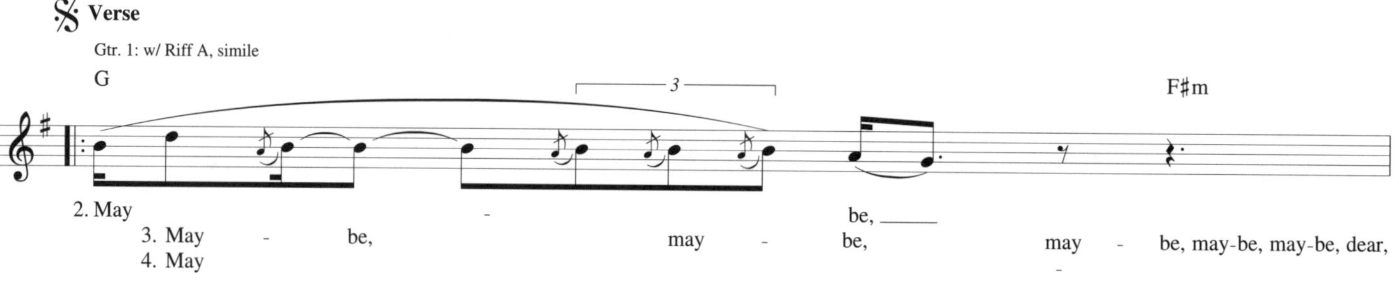
Verse
Gtr. 1: w/ Riff A, simile
G
F♯m
2. May - be,
3. May - be, may - be, may - be, may-be, may-be, dear,
4. May -

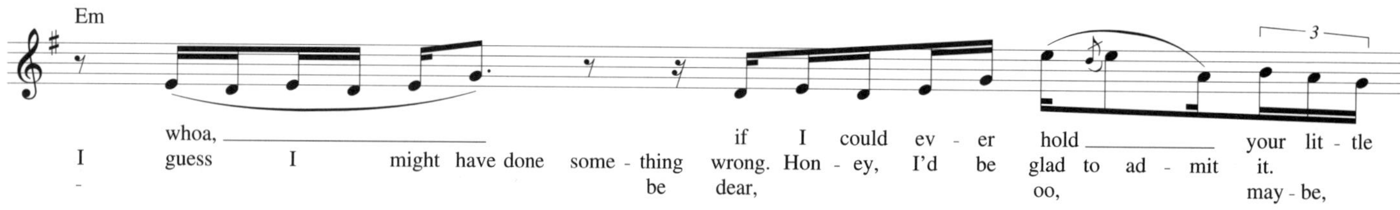
Em
whoa, if I could ev - er hold your lit - tle
I guess I might have done some - thing wrong. Hon - ey, I'd be glad to ad - mit it.
- be dear, oo, may - be,

3rd time, To Coda
Am
C
Bm
Am
D7
hand, oo, you might un - der - stand.
Oo, come on home to me. Hon - ey,
may - be, may - be, let me help you. Show me how. Hon - ey,

Chorus
G
C
1.
G
F♯m
May - be, may - be, may - be, may - be, yeah.
(May - be, may - be, may - be.)
Gtr. 1
simile on repeat
let ring
let ring

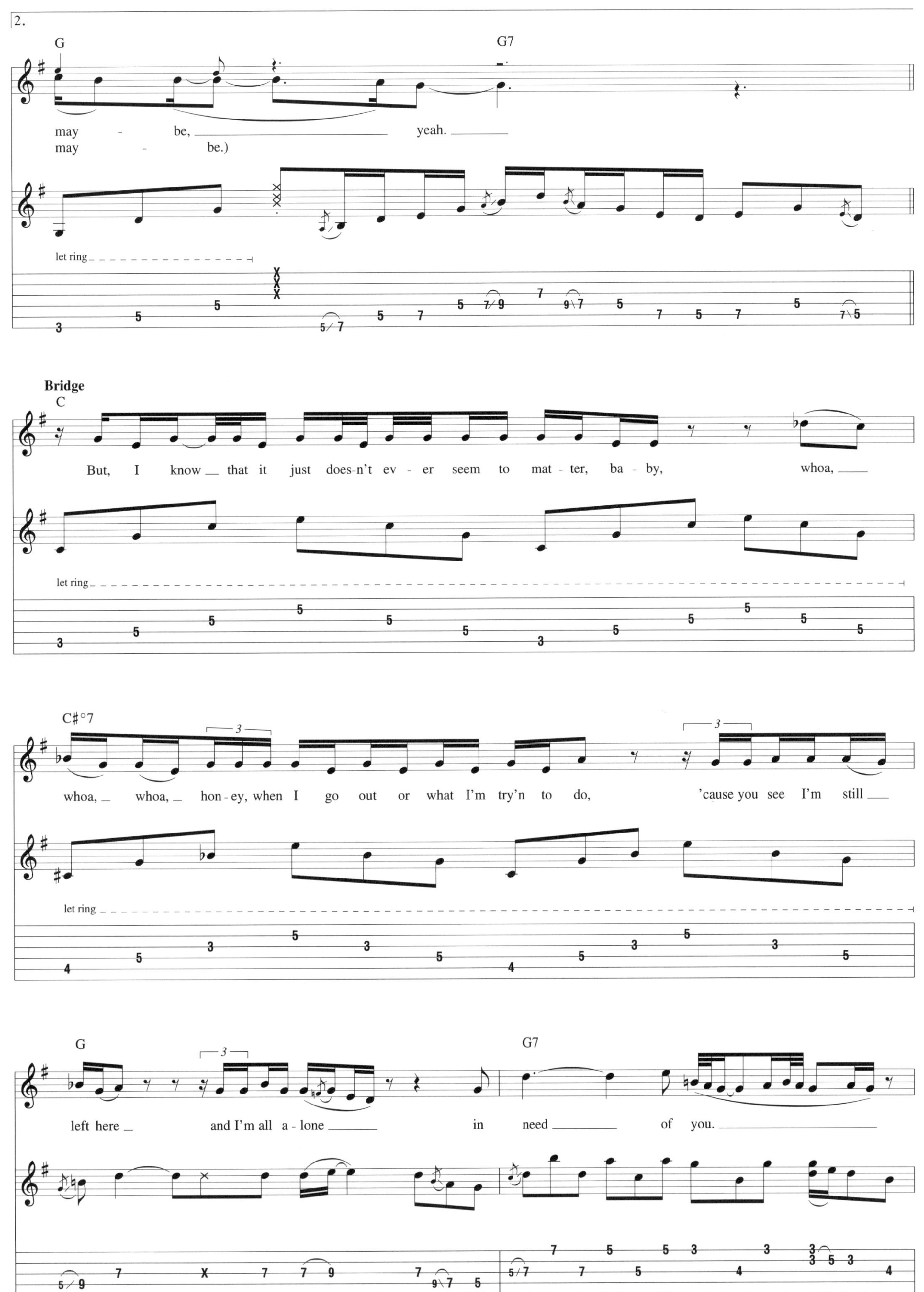
2.
G
G7
may - be, yeah.
may - be.)
let ring
Bridge
C
But, I know that it just does-n't ev - er seem to mat - ter, ba - by, whoa,
let ring
C♯°7
whoa, whoa, hon - ey, when I go out or what I'm try'n to do, 'cause you see I'm still
let ring
G
G7
left here and I'm all a - lone in need of you.

C
C♯°7
Please, please, please, please, oh, won't you re - con - sid-er, ba-by? Now, come on. I said you'd
let ring
let ring

G
E
Am
D7
come back. Won't you come back to me?

Interlude

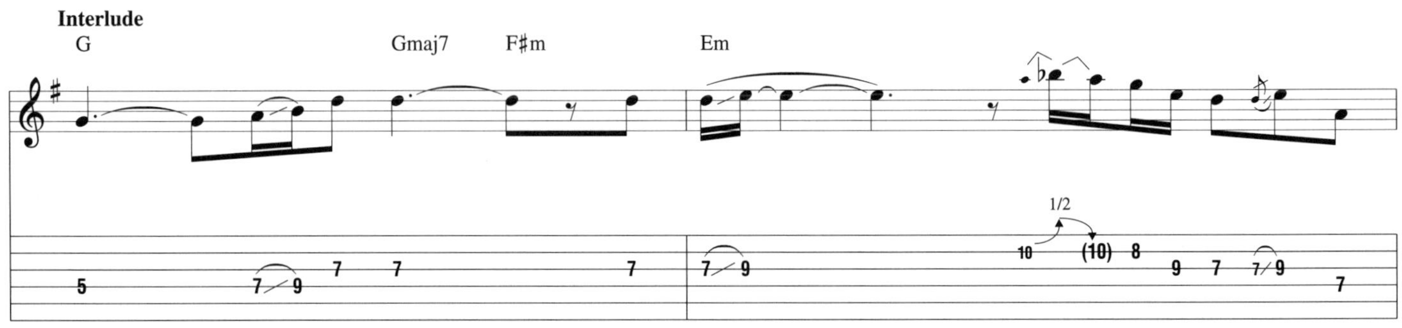
G
Gmaj7
F♯m
Em
1/2

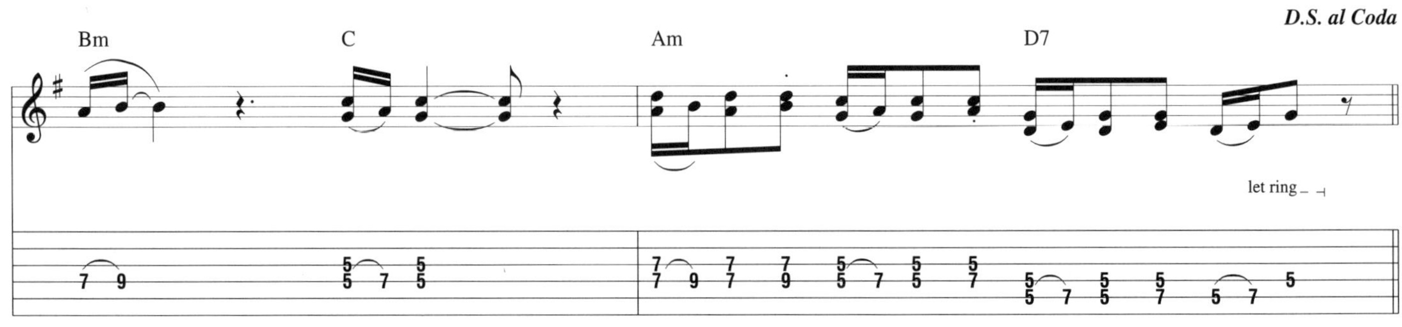
D.S. al Coda
Bm
C
Am
D7
let ring

Coda

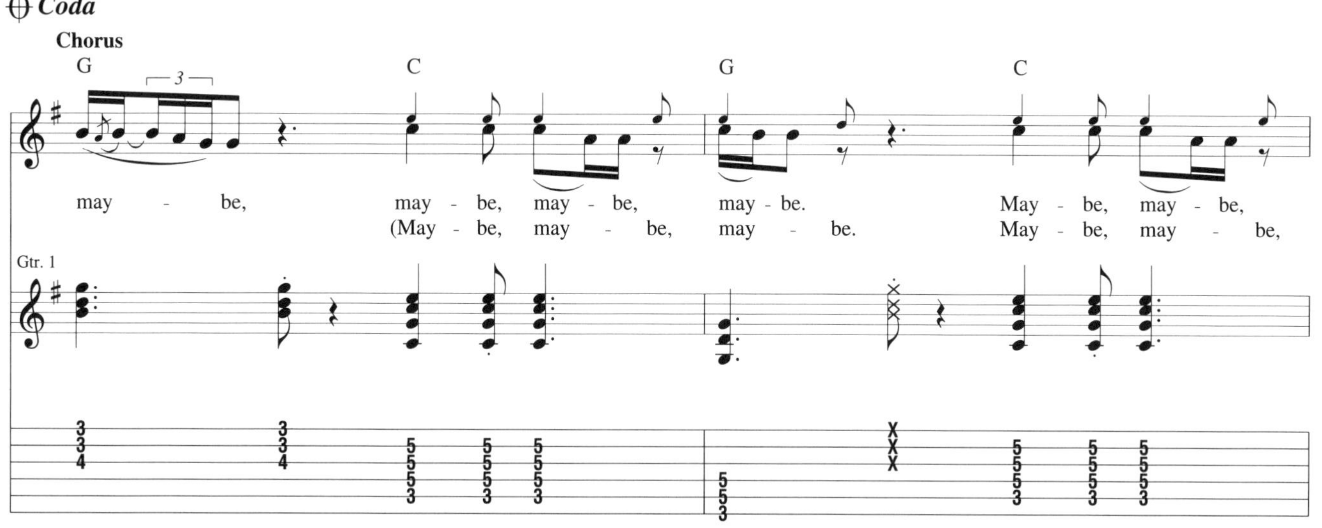
Chorus
G
C
G
C
may - be,
may - be, may - be,
may - be.
May - be, may - be,
(May - be, may - be,
may - be.
May - be, may - be,
Gtr. 1

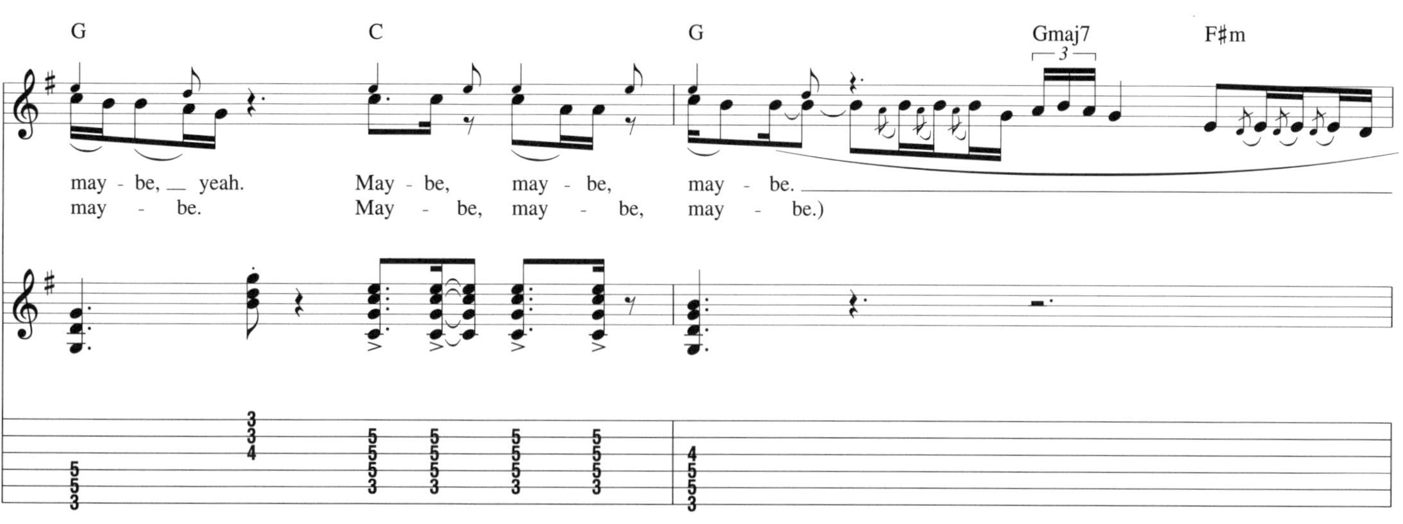
G
C
G
Gmaj7
F♯m
may - be, yeah.
May - be,
may - be,
may - be.
may - be.
May - be,
may - be,
may - be.)

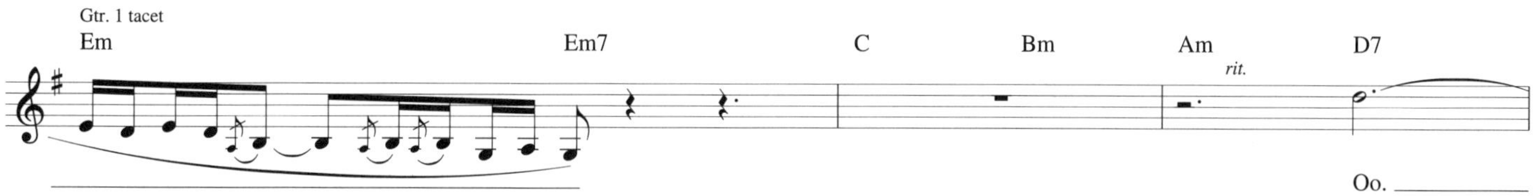
Gtr. 1 tacet
Em
Em7
C
Bm
Am
rit.
D7
Oo.

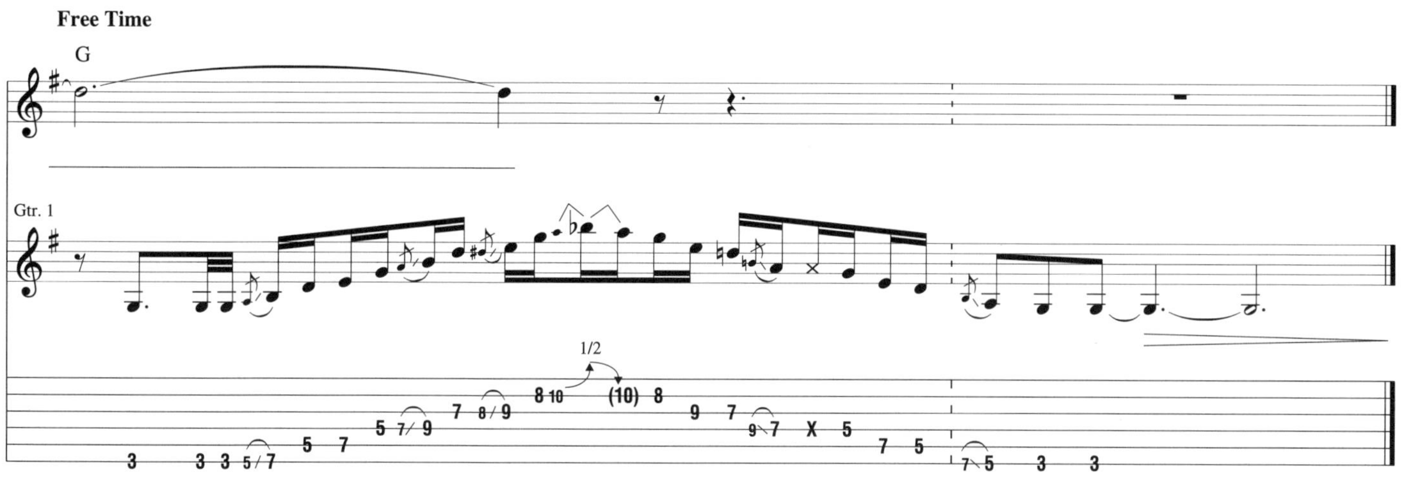
Free Time
G
Gtr. 1
1/2

from *Pearl*

Me and Bobby McGee

Words and Music by Kris Kristofferson and Fred Foster

* Quickly alternate between notes.

Gtr. 1: w/ Rhy. Fig. 1
G
was hold - in' Bob - by's hand in mine.
Gtr. 1: w/ Rhy. Fig. 2, 2 times, simile
D
We sang ev - 'ry song that driv - er knew.
Gtr. 2
let ring
Chorus
C
Gtr. 1
Free - dom's just an - oth - er word for
Gtr. 2
w/ pick & fingers
let ring
full
1/2
G
noth-in' left to lose.
D
Noth-in', don't mean noth - in', hon', if it ain't
free,
no, no,
C
If feel - in' good was eas - y, Lord,

Gtr. 1: w/ Rhy. Fig. 2, 3 times, simile
G
D
when he sang the blues, you know feel - in' good was good e - nough for me,
let ring
let ring
Gtr. 2
good e - nough for me and my Bob - by Mc -
w/ pick
let ring
Gtr. 1: w/ Rhy. Fig. 1
G
A
A
open
Rhy. Fig. 3
Gtr. 1
End Rhy. Fig. 3
Gee.
3. From the
Gtr. 2
1/2
Verse
Gtr. 1: w/ Rhy. Fig. 3, 3 times, simile
A
Ken - tuck - y coal mines to the Cal - i - for - nia sun, hey, Bob -
Gtr. 2
w/ pick & fingers

E
E
6
open
Rhy. Fig. 4
End Rhy. Fig. 4
Gtr. 1
by shared the se - crets of my soul.
Through all
Gtr. 2
w/ pick
let ring
Gtr. 1: w/ Rhy. Fig. 4, 3 times
kinds of weath - er, through ev - 'ry - thing that we've done, yeah,
Gtr. 2
let ring
Gtr. 1: w/ Rhy. Fig. 3
A
Bob-by, ba - by. helped me from the whole world.
4. One
full
Verse
Gtr. 1: w/ Rhy. Fig. 3, 2 1/2 times, simile
A
day up near Sal - i - nas, Lord, I let him slip a - way. He's
w/ pick & fingers
let ring

Gtr. 1: w/ Rhy. Fig. 2, 2 times, simile
A A7 D
open
Gtr. 1
look - in' for that home and I hope he finds it. But I'd
Gtr. 2
let ring
let ring
* Quickly alternate between notes.
Gtr. 1: w/ Rhy. Fig. 3
A
trade all of my to - mor - rows for one sin - gle yes - ter - day to be
Gtr. 2
let ring
let ring
Gtr. 1: w/ Rhy. Fig. 4
E E E
open
Gtr. 1
hold - in' Bob - by's bod - y next to mine.
Gtr. 2
w/ pick
Chorus
D A
Free - dom's just an - oth - er word for noth - in' left to lose.
w/ pick & fingers
let ring

E
A
Noth-in', that's all that Bob-by left me, yeah. But if
w/ pick
w/ pick & fingers w/ pick
w/ pick & fingers
full
D
A
feel-in' good was eas-y, Lord, when he sang the blues, hey,
let ring
let ring
Gtr. 1: w/ Rhy. Fig. 4, 3 times, simile
E
feel-in' good was good e-nough for me, mm, hmm,
Gtr. 2
let ring
w/ pick & fingers
* L. H. fingering
Gtr. 1: w/ Rhy. Fig. 3
A
good e-nough for me and my Bob-by Mc-Gee. La, da...
let ring
w/ pick
1/2

Interlude
Gtr. 1: w/ Rhy. Fig. 3, 3 times, simile
Gtr. 2 tacet
w/ Lead Voc. ad lib
Gtr. 1: w/ Rhy. Fig. 4, 4 times, simile
Gtr. 1: w/ Rhy. Fig. 3, simile
Interlude
Gtr. 1: w/ Rhy. Fig. 3, 3 times, simile
w/ Lead Voc. ad lib, 1st & 2nd times
Gtr. 2
w/ pick & fingers
let ring
simile on repeats
Gtr. 1: w/ Rhy. Fig. 4, 4 times, 1st & 3rd times
Gtr. 1: w/ Rhy. Fig. 4, 2nd & 4th times
Gtr. 1: w/ Fill 1, 2nd & 4th times, simile
Fill 1
Gtr. 2
8va
loco
w/ pick & fingers
let ring

1., 2., 3.
Gtr. 1: w/ Rhy. Fig. 3
A
let ring
w/ pick & fingers
hold bend
full
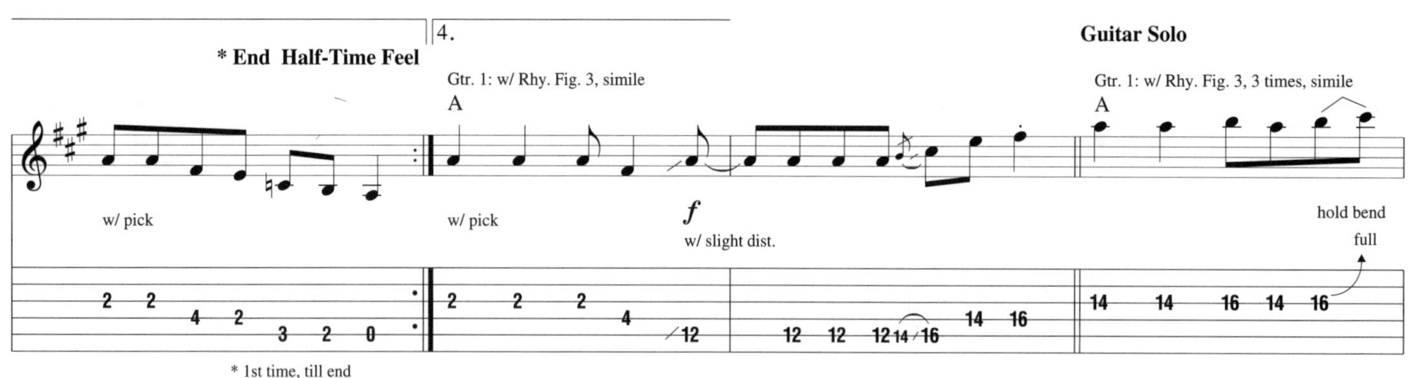
* End Half-Time Feel
4.
Gtr. 1: w/ Rhy. Fig. 3, simile
A
Guitar Solo
Gtr. 1: w/ Rhy. Fig. 3, 3 times, simile
A
w/ pick
w/ pick
f
w/ slight dist.
hold bend
full
* 1st time, till end
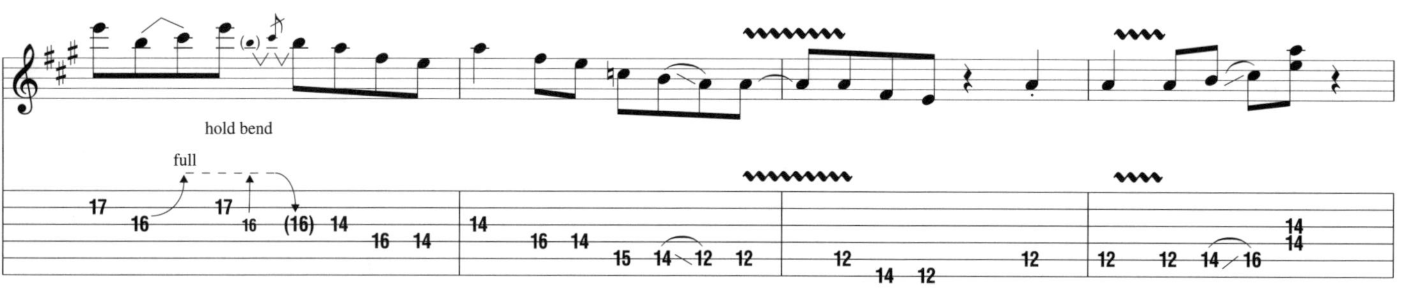
hold bend
full
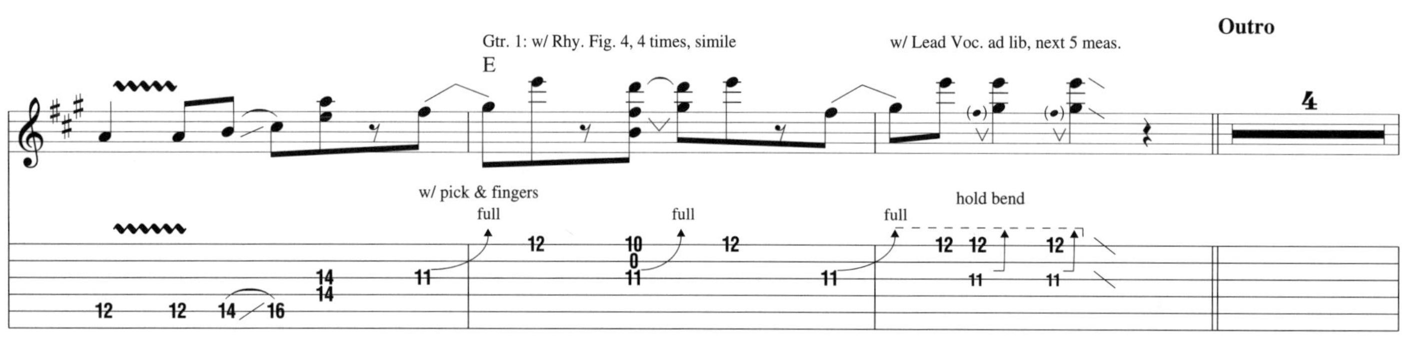
Gtr. 1: w/ Rhy. Fig. 4, 4 times, simile
E
w/ Lead Voc. ad lib, next 5 meas.
Outro
4
w/ pick & fingers
full
full
full
hold bend

N.C.
A
Hey, hey, hey, Bob-by Mc-Gee, yeah.
mf
w/ clean tone & pick
** Strum in eighth note rhythm while sliding (beats 1 & 2 only)

from *Pearl*

Mercedes Benz

Words and Music by Janis Joplin, Michael McClure and Bob Neuwirth

from *Pearl*

Move Over

Words and Music by Janis Joplin

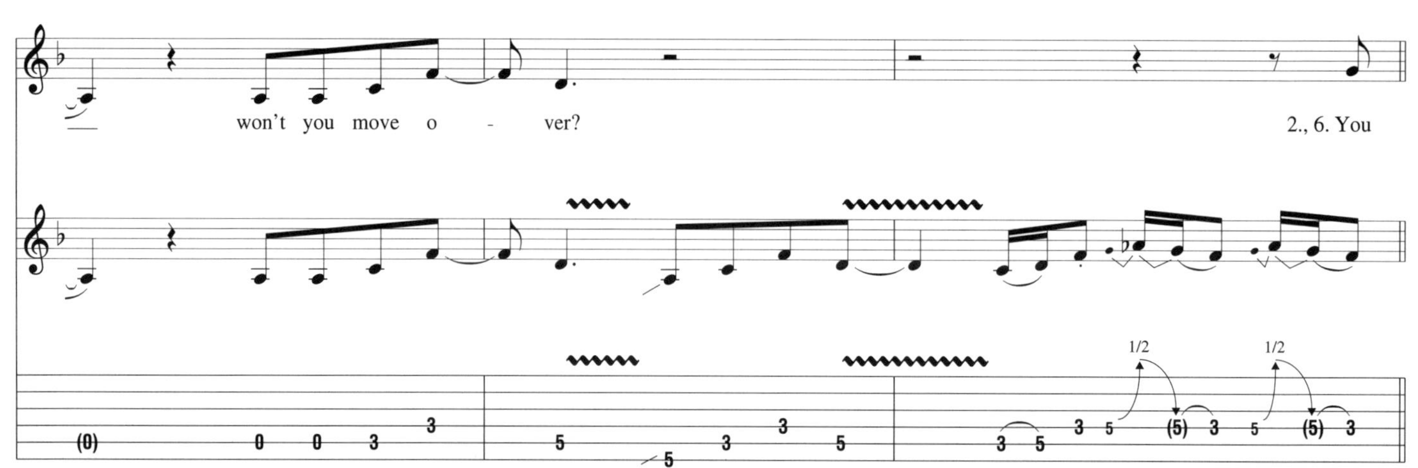

Verse
Gtr. 1: w/ Riff A, 1st time
Gtr. 2: w/ Riff B, 2nd time, simile
know that I need a man 1. now, Lord. 5. hon-ey told ya so.
You know that I need a man. But when I

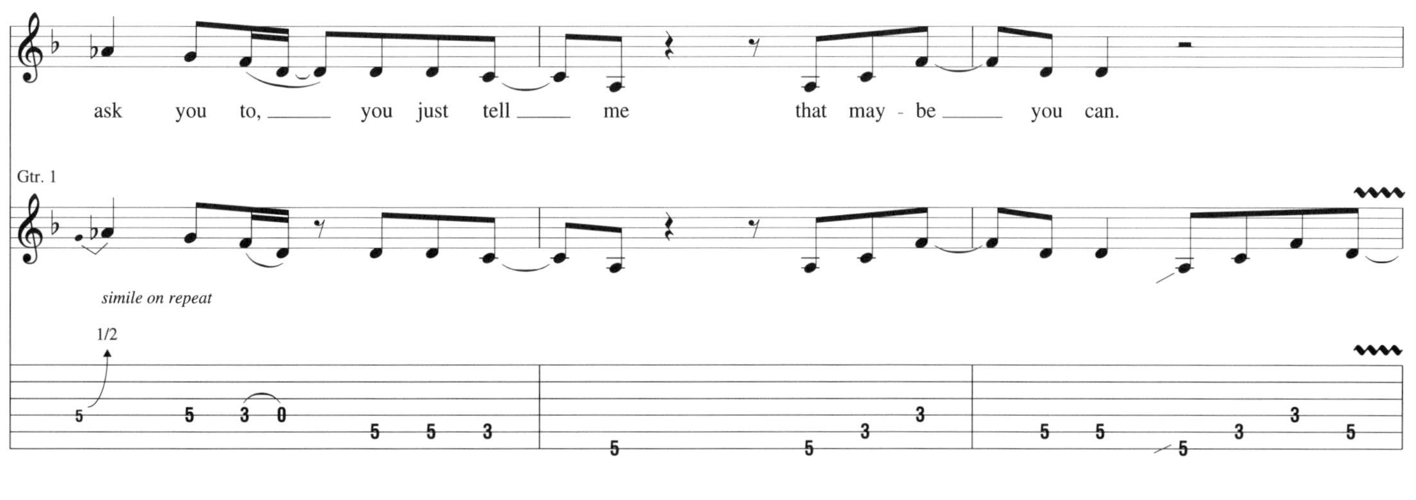
ask you to, you just tell me that may-be you can.
Gtr. 1
simile on repeat
1/2

w/ Lead Voc. ad lib, 2nd time
Verse
N.C.
F G
3.,7. Please don't you do it to me, babe, no.
ain't quite a read-y for walk-in' no,no,no, no. I
Riff B
simile on repeats
1/2

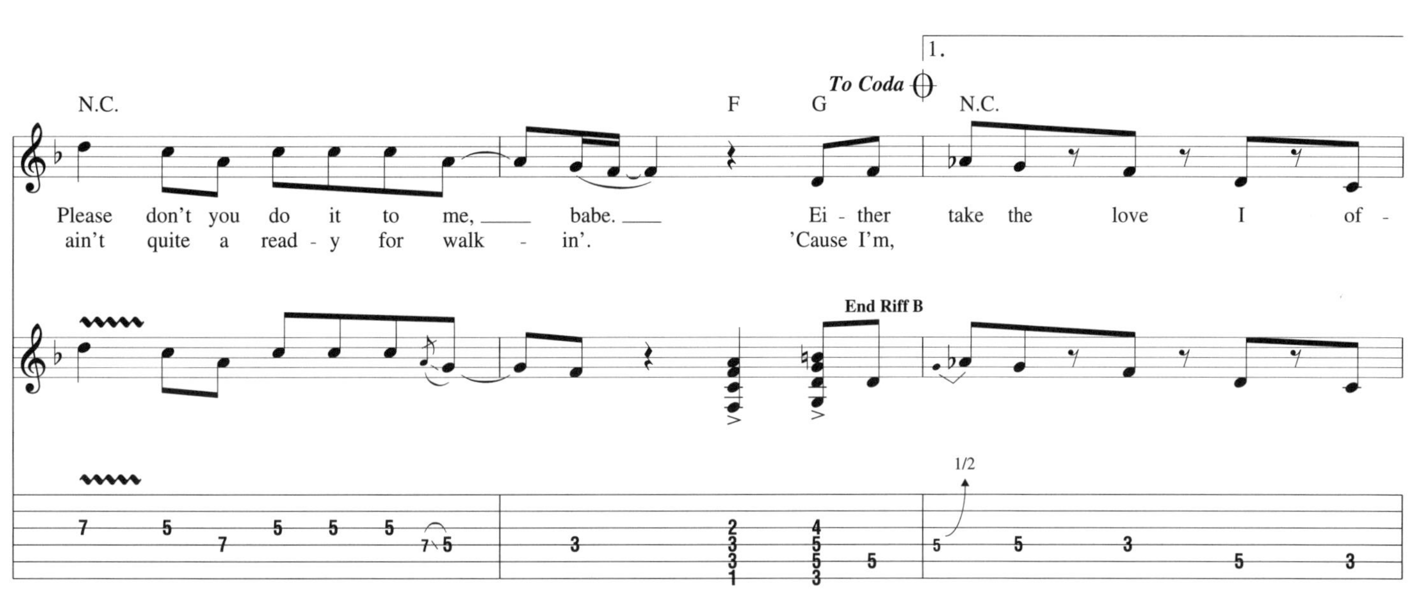
1.
To Coda
N.C.
F G
N.C.
Please don't you do it to me, babe. Ei-ther take the love I of-
ain't quite a read-y for walk-in'. 'Cause I'm,
End Riff B
1/2

fer or just let me be.
4. I
1/2
2.
dog - gone it, through with your lie,
Lord I'm just dan - gl - in'.
1/2
Bridge
D5 D♯5 E7♯9
E5
Oh, yeah. Make up your mind, hon - ey,
steady gliss.
G
E7♯9
you're play - in' with me. Yeah, yeah. Make up your mind,
steady gliss.

* Chord symbols reflect basic tonality, next 18 meas.

rake
1/2
1/2

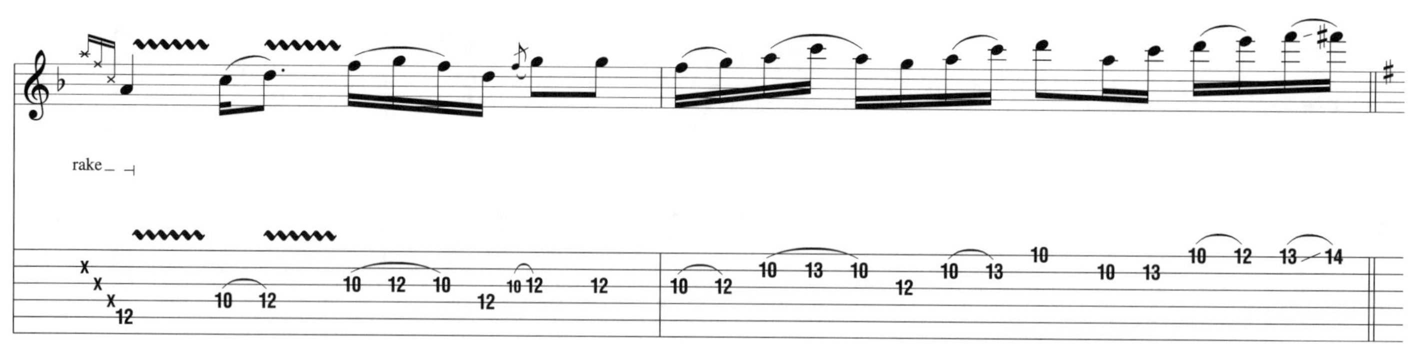
rake

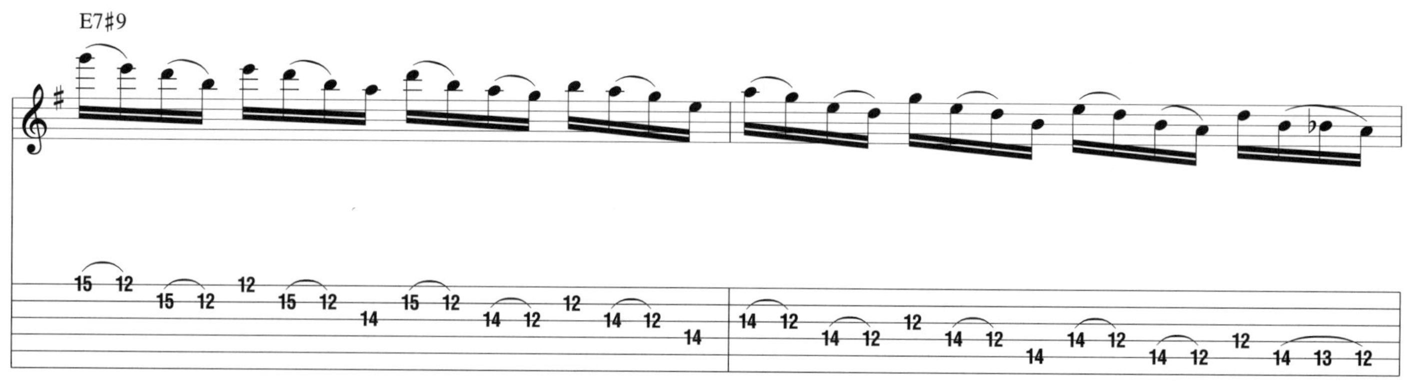
E7#9

G
E7#9
full

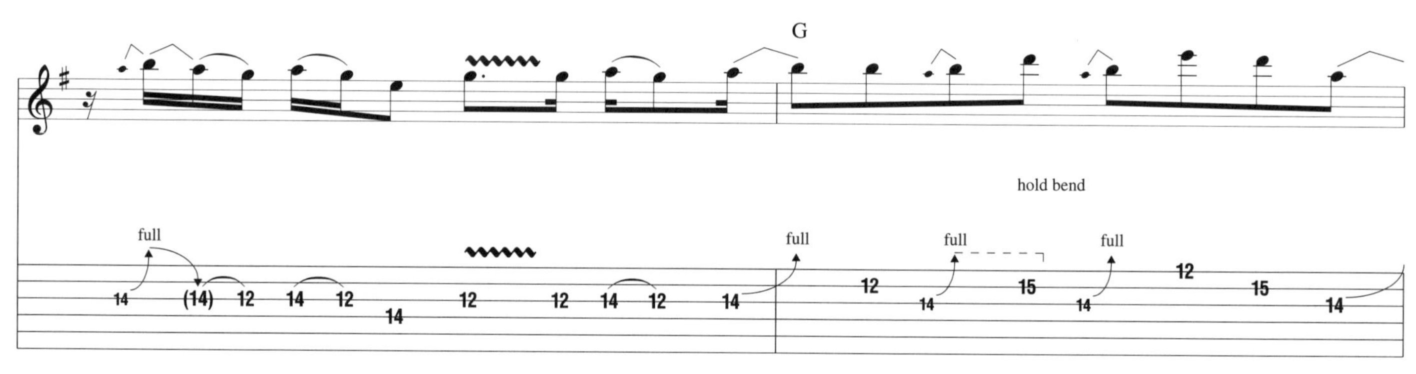
G
hold bend
full
full
full
full

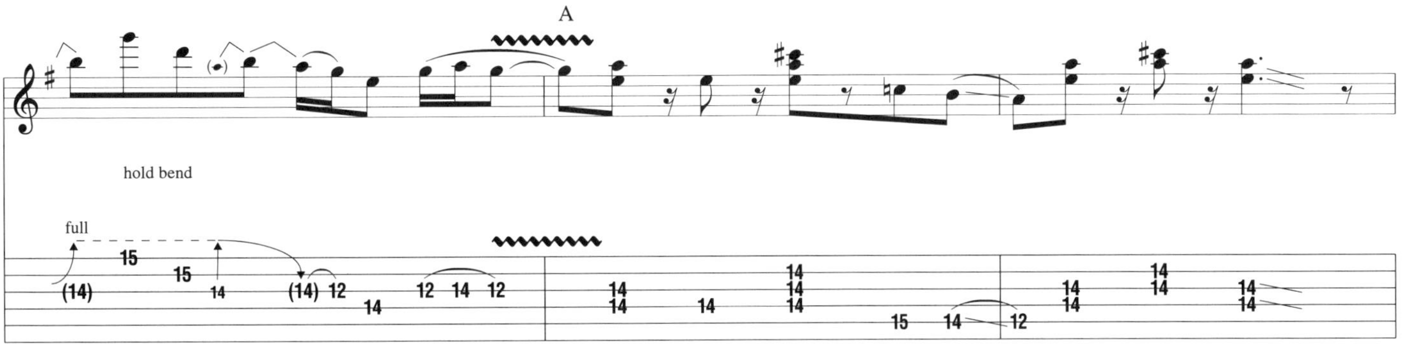
A
hold bend
full
1/2

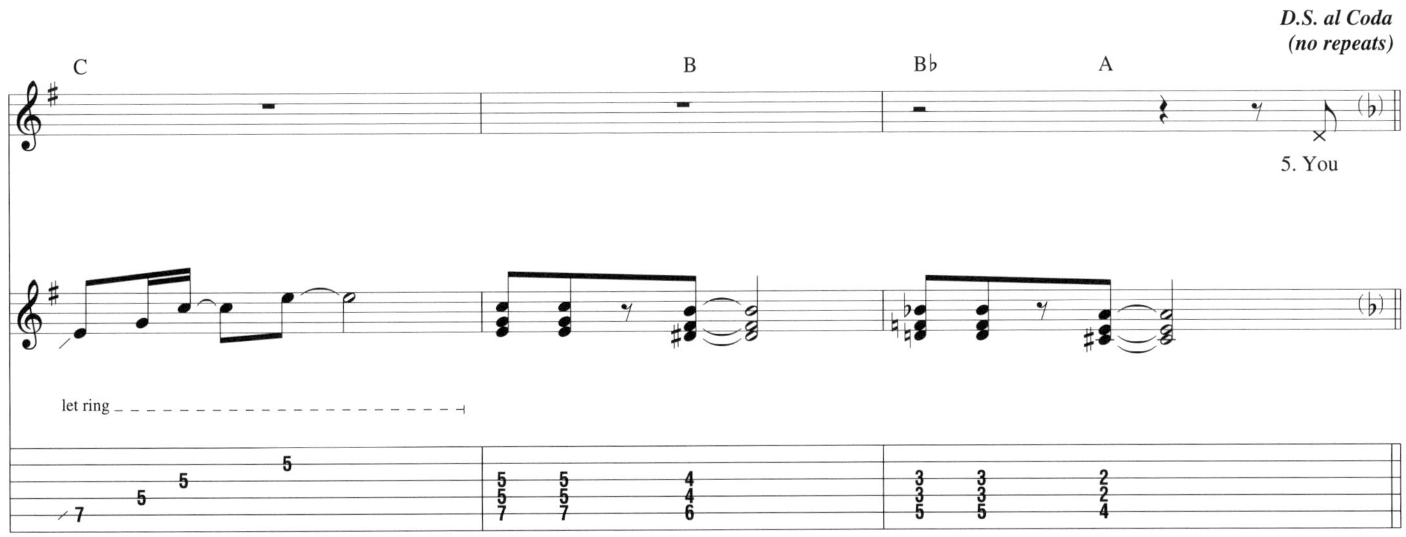
D.S. al Coda
(no repeats)
C
B
B♭
A
5. You
let ring

Coda
N.C.
take the love I of - fer, hon', or let me be.
1/2

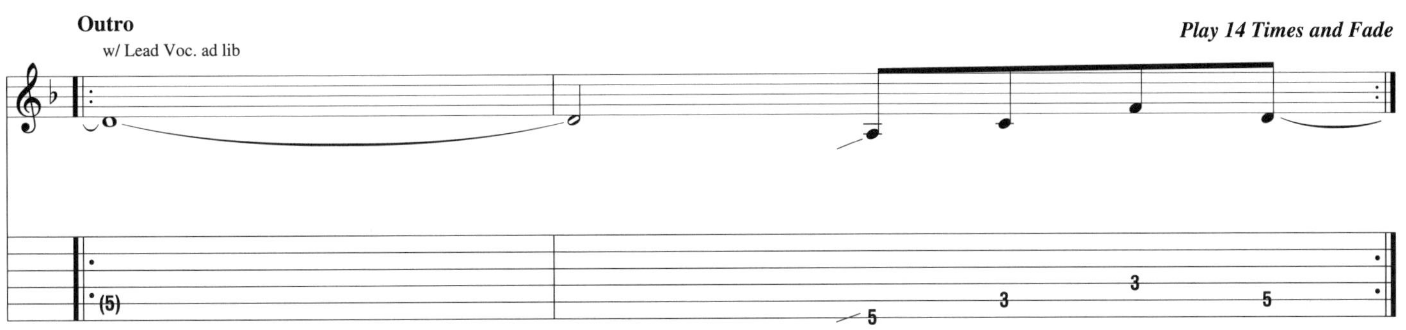
Outro
w/ Lead Voc. ad lib
Play 14 Times and Fade

from *I Got Dem Ol' Kosmic Blues Again Mama!*

One Good Man

Words and Music by Janis Joplin

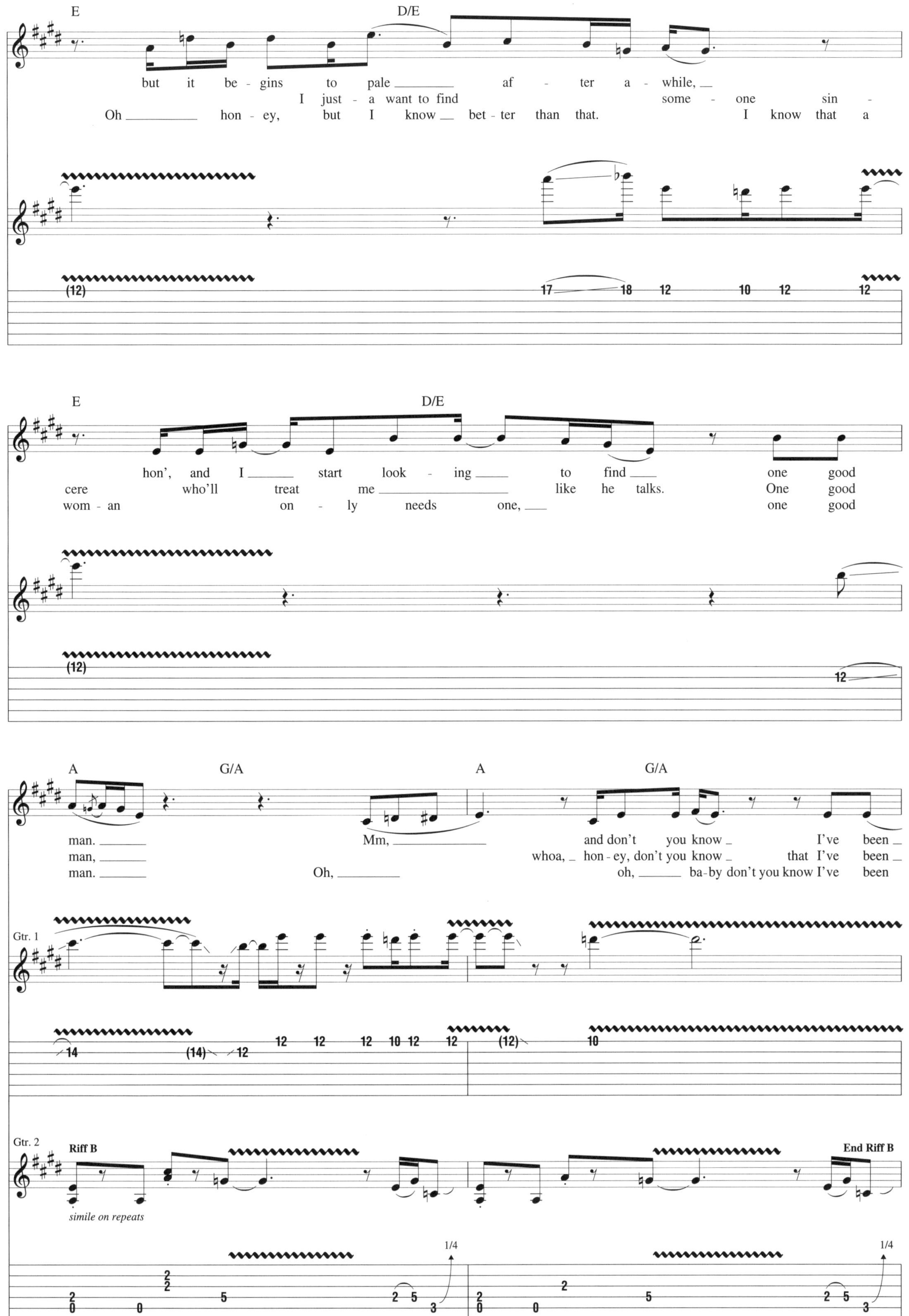
E
D/E
but it be - gins to pale af - ter a - while,
I just - a want to find some - one sin -
Oh hon - ey, but I know bet - ter than that. I know that a
(12)
17 18 12 10 12 12
E
D/E
hon', and I start look - ing to find one good
cere who'll treat me like he talks. One good
wom - an on - ly needs one, one good
(12)
12
A
G/A
A
G/A
man. Mm, and don't you know I've been
man, whoa, hon - ey, don't you know that I've been
man. Oh, oh, ba - by don't you know I've been
Gtr. 1
14 (14) 12 12 12 12 10 12 12 (12) 10
Gtr. 2
Riff B
End Riff B
simile on repeats
1/4
1/4

Gtr. 2: w/ Riff A, simile
E
D/E
E
D/E
search - ing.
look - ing.
look - ing.
Oo,
yes I have.
Oh,
Mm,
one good
one
Gtr. 1
B
A/B
A
G/A
Uh, one good man,
oh,
ain't
much,
hon', ain't much,
it's on - ly
man
ain't
much,
hon', it ain't much, oh,
it's on - ly
good man,
it ain't much, no, no,
hon', it ain't much,
oh, it's on - ly
Gtr. 1
Gtr. 2
Riff C
End Riff C
simile on repeats
1.
2.
Gtr. 2: w/ Riff A, simile
To Coda
E
D/E
E
D/E
E
D/E
ev - 'ry - thing.
ev - 'ry - thing.
ev - 'ry lit - tle thing,
just-a ev-'ry-thing,
Mm, whoa, yeah.
Oh,
all right.
Gtr. 1
w/ o slide
full
1/4

Guitar Solo

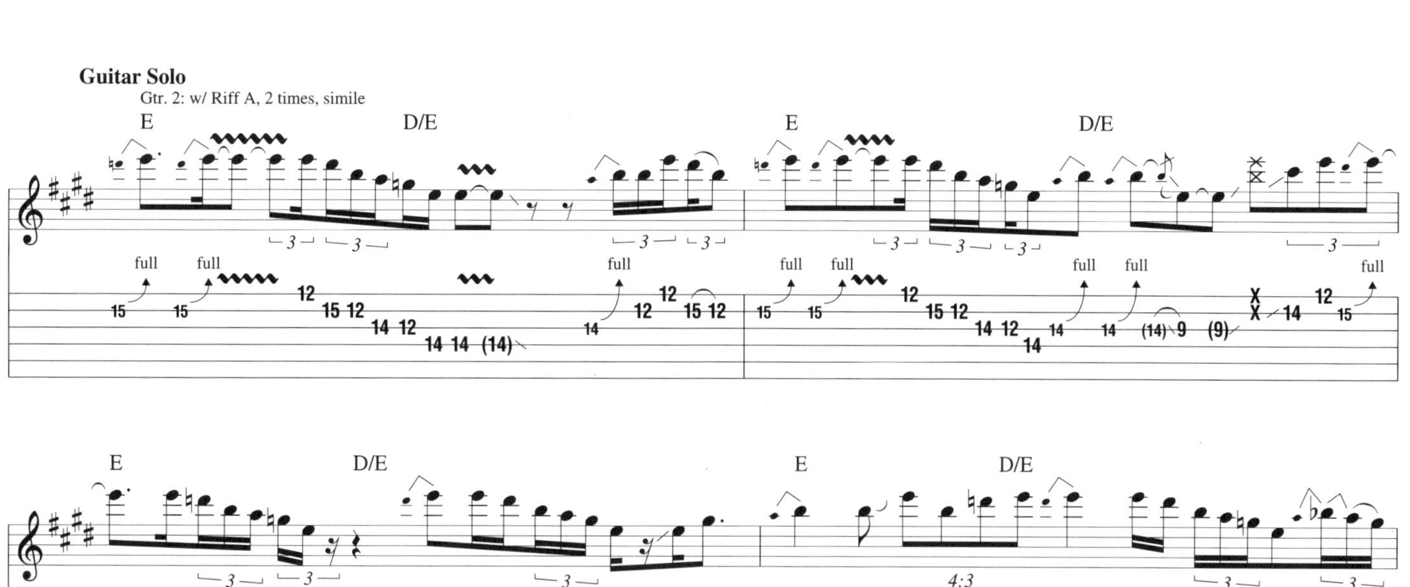
Gtr. 2: w/ Riff A, 2 times, simile
E
D/E
E
D/E
full
full
full
full
full
full
full
full

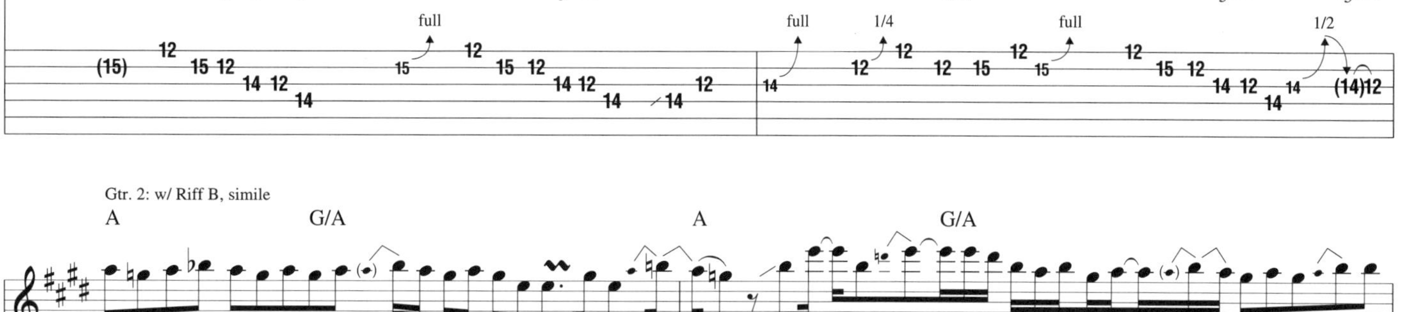
E
D/E
E
D/E
full
full
1/4
full
1/2

Gtr. 2: w/ Riff B, simile
A
G/A
A
G/A
1/2
full
full
full
full

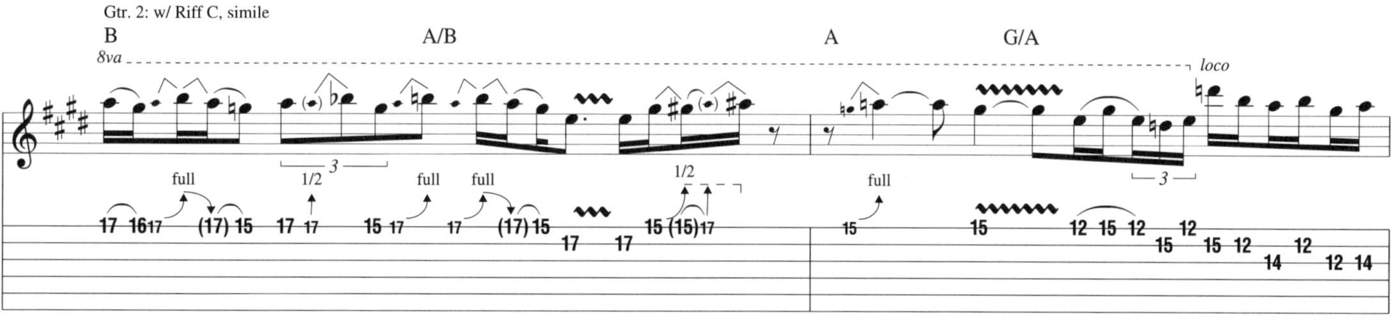
Gtr. 2: w/ Riff A, simile
E
D/E
E
D/E
8va
full
1/2
* 1/2
* hold bend while executing hammer-on.
Gtr. 2: w/ Riff C, simile
B
A/B
A
G/A
8va
loco
full
1/2
full
full
1/2
full

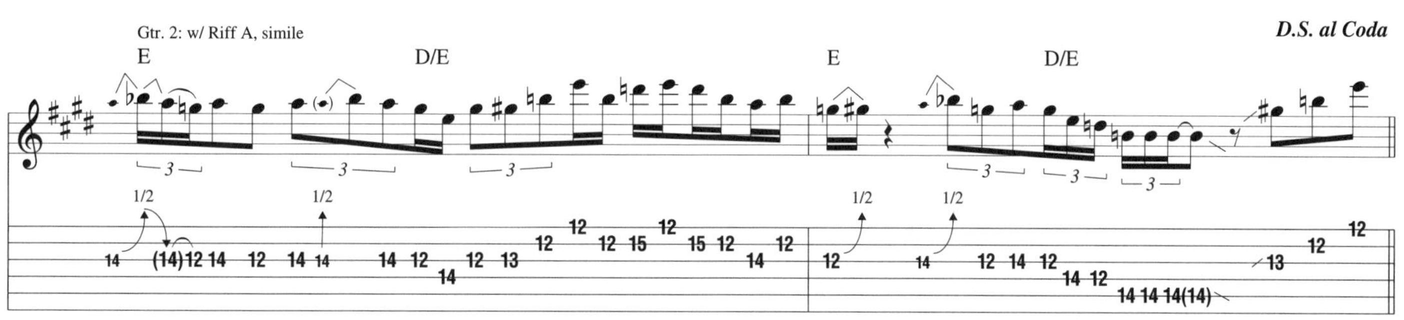
Gtr. 2: w/ Riff A, simile
D.S. al Coda
E
D/E
E
D/E
1/2
1/2
1/2
1/2

Coda
Outro
E
D/E
ev - 'ry-thing.
Oh,
yeah.
Gtr. 1
w/ o slide
full
Gtr. 2
Gtr. 2 tacet
Begin Fade
8va
Fade Out

Piece of My Heart

Words and Music by Jerry Ragovoy and Bert Berns

Verse

E A

come __ on, come __ on, come __ on, come __ on. 1. Did-n't I make you feel __________

out on the streets look-in'

simile on repeat

let ring

mf *simile on repeat*

tr tr

B A E A

like you ________________ were the on - ly man? _

good, _ and ba - by, deep down in your heart _ I guess ya know that it ain't right.

mp

tr tr

B A E A

Well, yeah, ___ and did - n't I give you near - ly ev - 'ry - thing that a wom - an

Now, but now, but now, but now, but now, but now, ___ but hear ___ me when I cry ___ at night. ___

tr tr

B

Pre-Chorus

C♯m

pos - si - bly can? _ Hon - ey, you know I ____ did. ______ And each time I tell __ my - self __ that I,

_______ Babe, and I cry all the time. ____________ But each time I tell __ my - self __ that I,

(Oh. ______

mf

f

B

when I think I've had e - nough. _ Oh, but I'm ___

when I can't stand the pain. ___ But, when you hold

D

gon - na show ya, ba - by, ______ that a

me in ___ your arms, ___________ I'm

Oh. ____

B

wom - an ___ can be tough. _ I want you to

sing - ing once a - gain. ______________ I said

come ______ on, come ________ on,

let ring _

Chorus

E A B A

Voc. Fig. 1

come __ on, come ____ on {and / yeah} take it. Take an-oth-er lit-tle piece of my heart, _ now, ba - by. ______

(Take it. Oh, ______

Rhy. Fig. 1

f

P.M.

Rhy. Fig. 1A

let ring

let ring

E A B A

Break an-oth-er lit-tle bit off my heart, __ now, dar - lin' yeah, _____ yeah, yeah, yeah. _

break it. Oh, __________

P.M.

let ring

E A B B♭ A

End Voc. Fig. 1

Have an-oth-er lit-tle piece of my heart, __ now, ba - by. __ Well, you know you got _ it if it

have a...)

End Rhy. Fig. 1

P.M.

End Rhy. Fig. 1A

tr

E F♯m E 1. E A B A

makes you feel good, _ oh, yes in - deed. _ 2. You're

tr

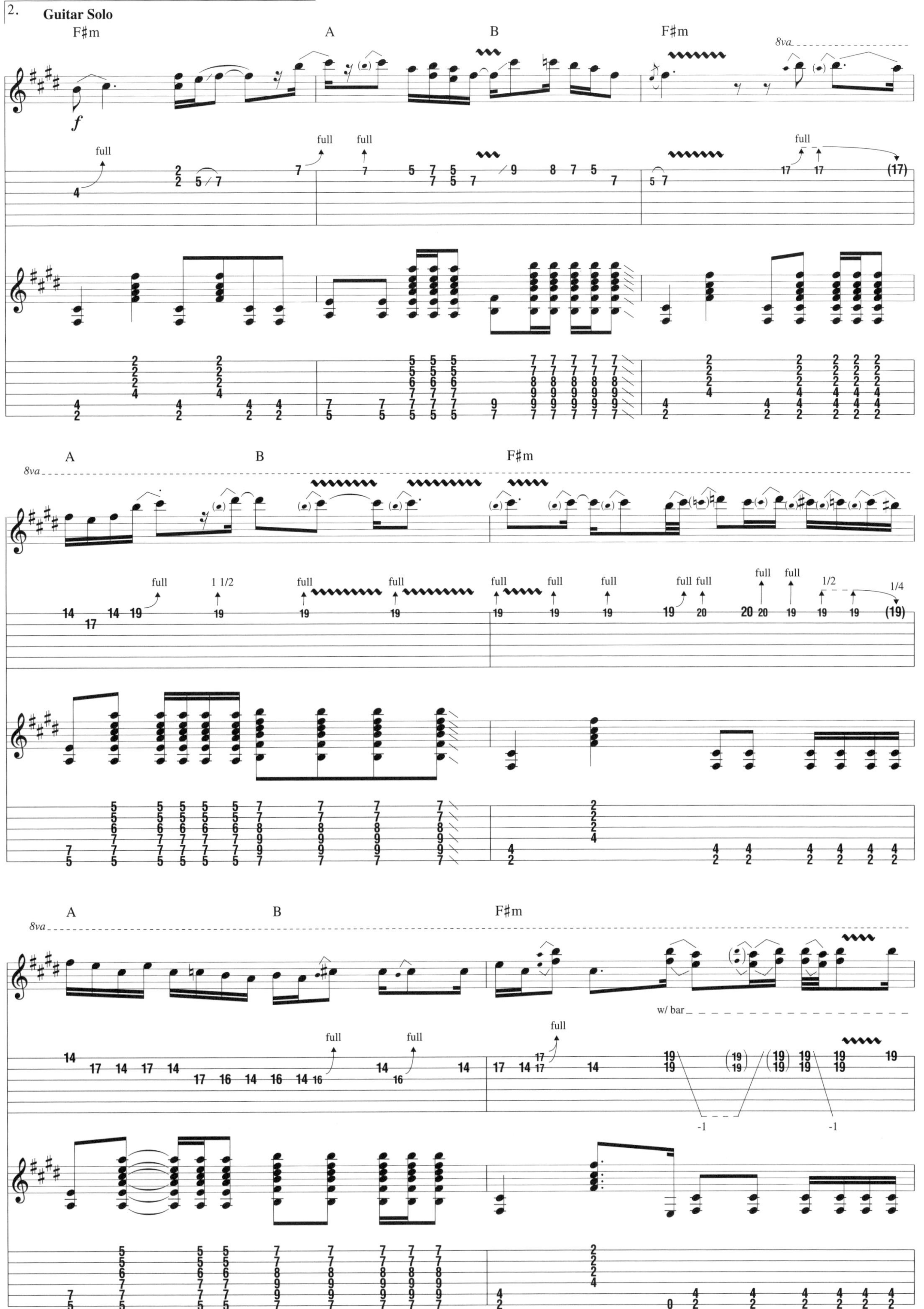

2.
Guitar Solo
F♯m
A
B
F♯m
8va
full
full
full
full
A
B
F♯m
8va
full
1 1/2
full
full
full
full
full
full
full
full
full
1/2
1/4
A
B
F♯m
8va
w/ bar
full
full
full
-1
-1

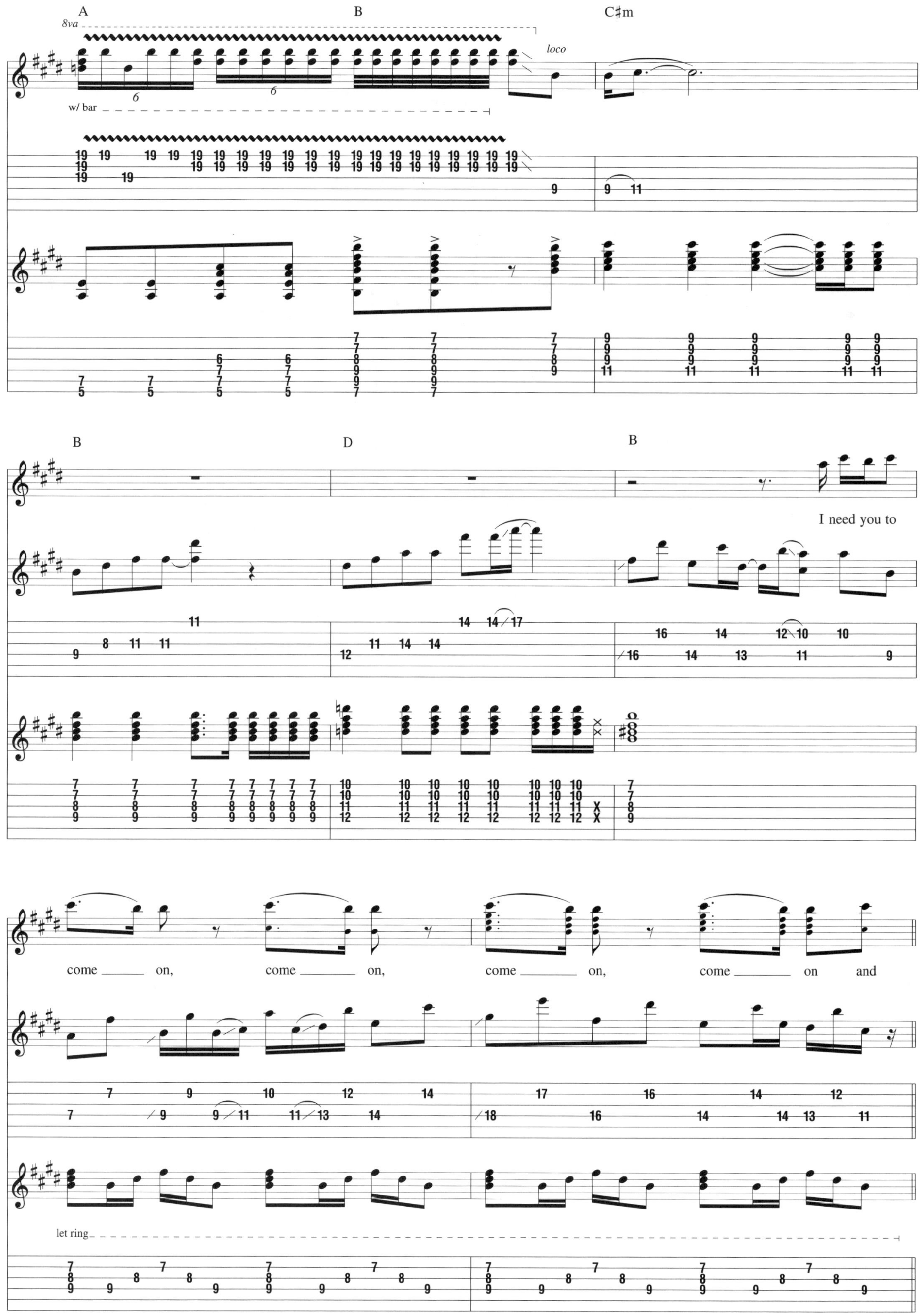
A
B
C♯m
8va
loco
w/ bar
B
D
B
I need you to
come on, come on, come on, come on and
let ring

Chorus

Gtrs. 1 & 2: w/ Rhy. Figs. 1 & 1A, simile
Bkgd. Voc.: w/ Voc. Fig. 1
E
A
B
A
take it. Take an - oth - er lit - tle piece of my heart, now, ba - by.

E
A
B
A
Break an - oth - er lit - tle bit off my heart, now, dar - lin', yeah, come on now.

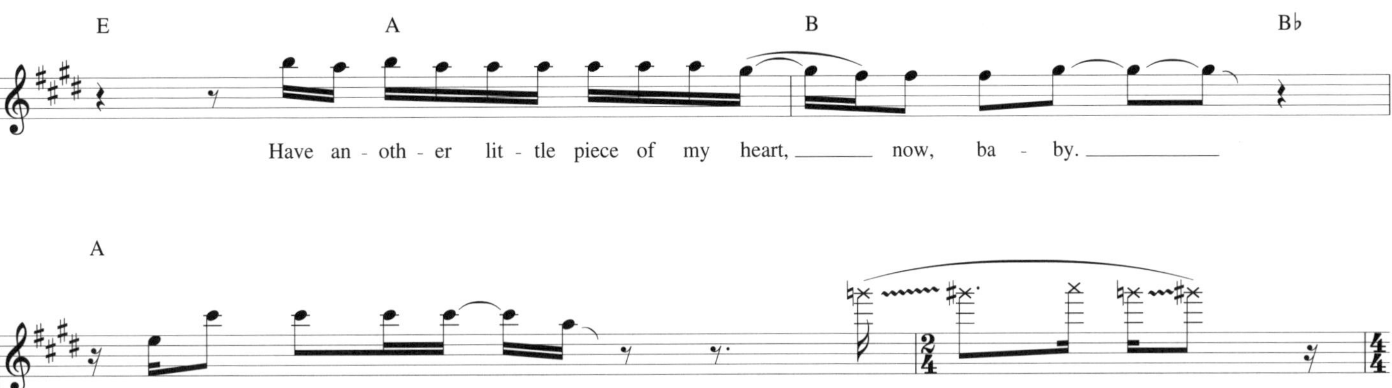
E
A
B
B♭
Have an - oth - er lit - tle piece of my heart, now, ba - by.

A
Uh, you know you got it. Wah,
Gtr. 1
5
5
6
7
7
5
Gtr. 2
5
5
6
7

Gtrs. 1 & 2: w/ Rhy. Figs. 1 & 1A, simile
Bkgd. Voc.: w/ Voc. Fig. 1
E
A
B
A
take it! Take an - oth - er lit - tle piece of my heart, now, ba - by.

E
A
B
A
Break an - oth - er lit - tle bit off my heart, now, dar - lin', yeah, yeah, yeah.
E
A
B
B♭
Have an - oth - er lit - tle piece of my heart, now, ba - by.
A
E F♯m E
F♯m
Well, you know you got it, sure e-nough, it makes you feel good.
(...makes you feel good.)
Gtr. 1
grad. bend
full
Gtr. 2
A
B
F♯m
8va
rit.
fdbk.
dim.
pitch: A♯
rit.
fdbk.
dim.
pitch: F♯

from *Cheap Thrills*

Summertime

from PORGY AND BESS®

By George Gershwin, Du Bose and Dorothy Heyward and Ira Gershwin

* Chord symbols reflect implied tonality.

* Gtr. 1 to left of slashes in TAB.

Verse
Gm
Gm(maj7)/F♯
Gtr. 2 tacet
Gm7/F
C7♭9
F9sus4
time, time, time, child, the liv - in's
morn - ings you're gon - na rise,
* Riff A
let ring
Gtr. 1
End Riff A
** simile on repeat
* refers to Gtr. 1 only
** Gtr. 2 tacet on D.S.
Gm
Gm(maj7)/F♯
Gm7/F
Gtr. 1: w/ Fill 1, 2nd time
C7
F7sus4
Cm
eas - y. Fish are jump - in'
rise up sing - ing. You're gon - na spread your
Gtr. 2 divisi
Riff B
full
End Riff B
Gtr. 1 tacet, 1st time
Gtr. 1: w/ Fill 2, 2nd time
Cm(maj7)
Cm7
C7
D5
now. Hey, the cot-ton, Lord, cot - ton's high,
wings, child, and take, take to the sky,
(cont. in slash)
8va
f w/ dist.
Fill 2
* grad. release
1/2
* ② str. caught under bend finger.
loco
dist. off

E♭5
D5
Cm
B♭
Am
Lord, so high.
Lord, the sky.
2. Your dad - dy's
4. Un - til the
8va
full
dist. off
Verse
Gtr. 1: w/ Riff A
Gtr. 2 tacet
Gm
Gm(maj7)/F♯
Gm7/F
C7♭9
F9sus4
rich
morn - ing,
and your
hon - ey,
ma's
n
s -
Gtr. 2: w/ Riff B
C7
so good - look - in', babe.
noth - in's go - in' to harm you now.
She's look - in' good now.
No, no, no, no, no,
Gtr. 1
let ring
Fill 1
To Coda
F7sus4
B♭ VI
Gtr. 2
no, no, no, no, no, no, no, no, no, no.
Hush, ba - by, ba - by, ba - by, ba - by, ba -
End Fill 1

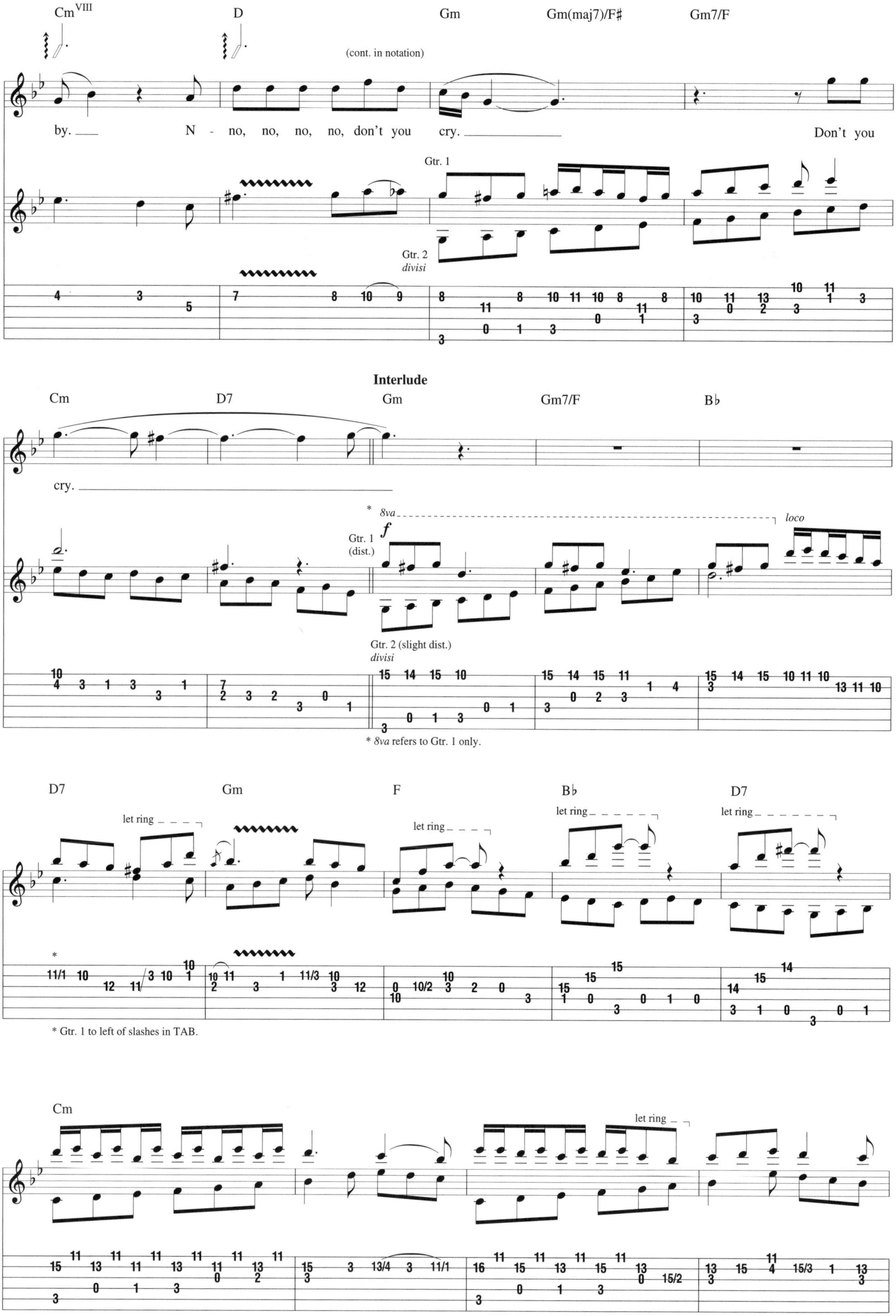

Cm[VIII] D Gm Gm(maj7)/F♯ Gm7/F

(cont. in notation)

by. N - no, no, no, no, don't you cry. Don't you

Gtr. 1

Gtr. 2
divisi

Interlude

Cm D7 Gm Gm7/F B♭

cry.

* *8va*

f

Gtr. 1 (dist.)

loco

Gtr. 2 (slight dist.)
divisi

* *8va* refers to Gtr. 1 only.

D7 Gm F B♭ D7

let ring

let ring

let ring

let ring

* Gtr. 1 to left of slashes in TAB.

D7
E♭7
D7
C5

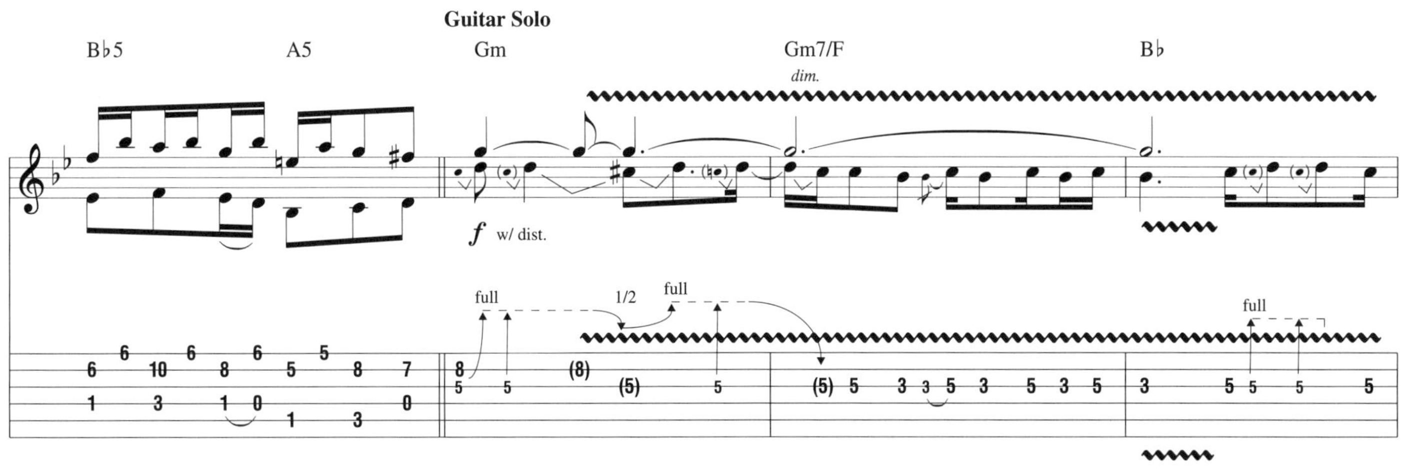
Guitar Solo
B♭5
A5
Gm
Gm7/F
B♭
dim.
f w/ dist.
full
1/2
full
full

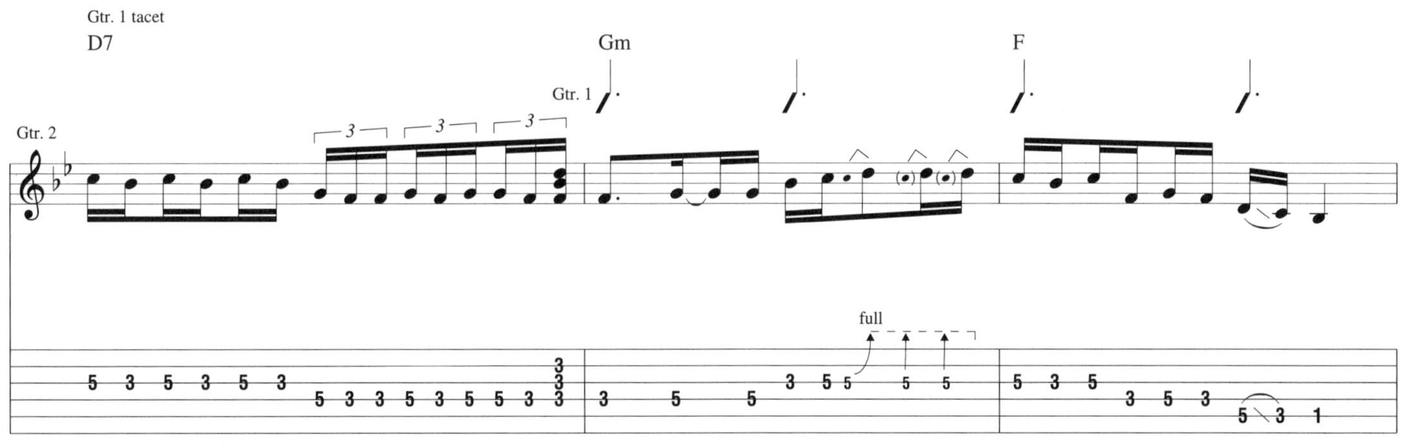
Gtr. 1 tacet
D7
Gm
F
Gtr. 1
Gtr. 2
full

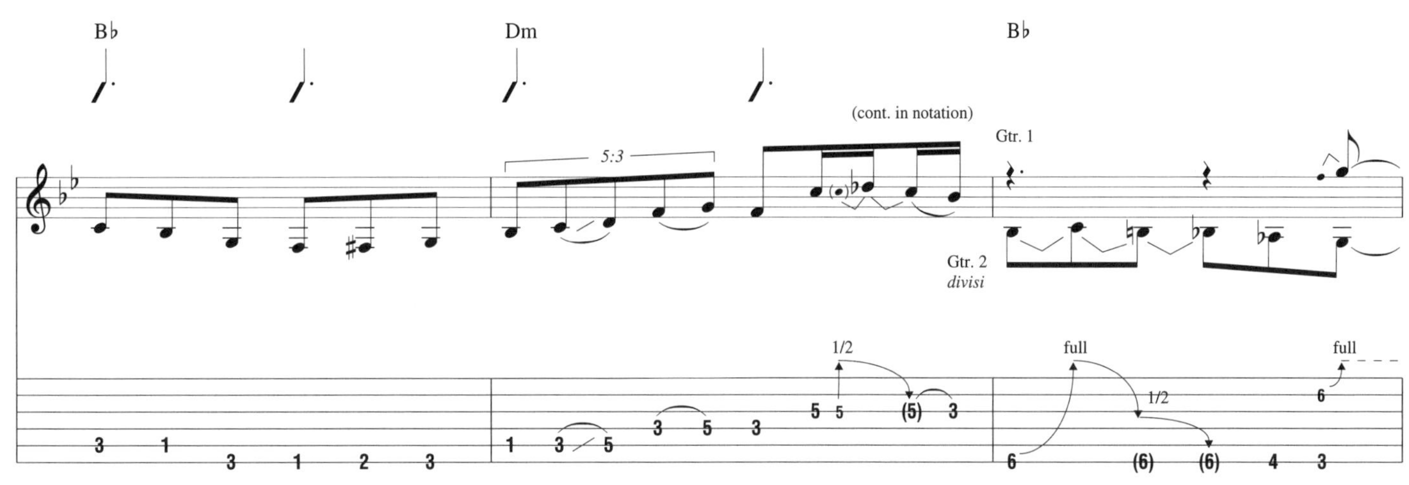
B♭
Dm
B♭
(cont. in notation)
Gtr. 1
Gtr. 2
divisi
5:3
1/2
full
1/2
full

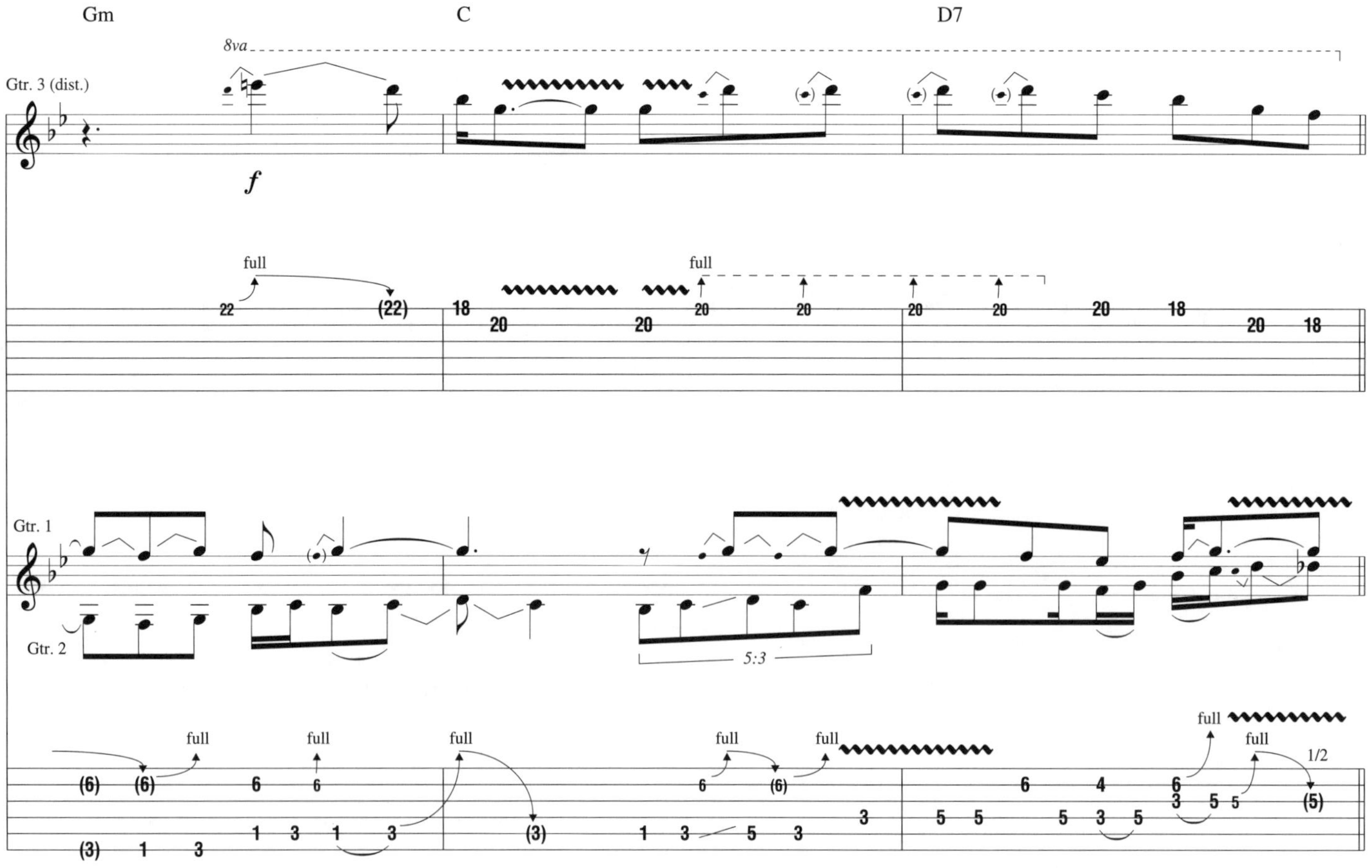

Gm C D7

8va

Gtr. 3 (dist.)

f

full full

Gtr. 1

Gtr. 2

5:3

full full full full full full full 1/2

Interlude

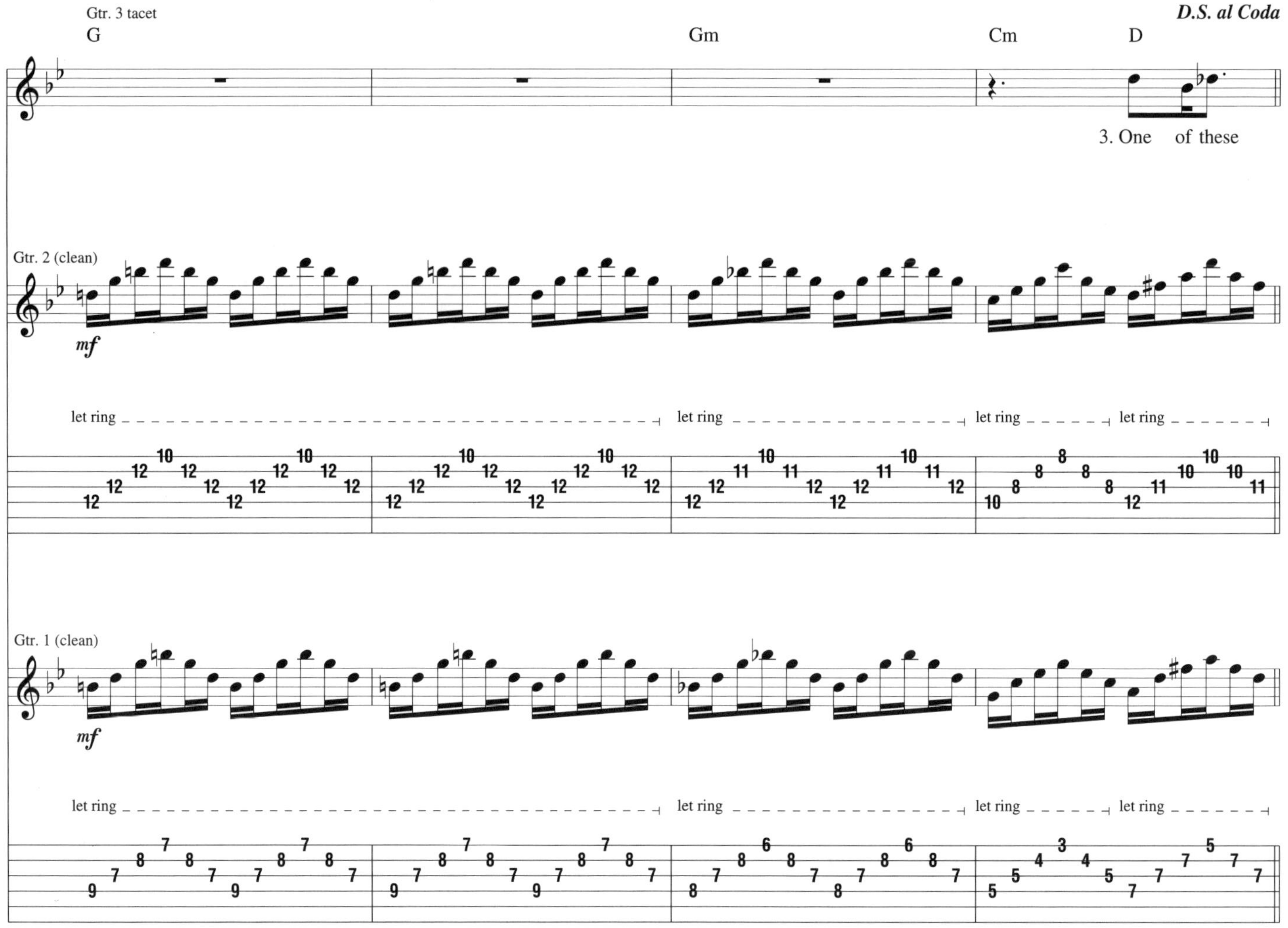

Gtr. 3 tacet

G Gm Cm D

D.S. al Coda

3. One of these

Gtr. 2 (clean)

mf

let ring let ring let ring let ring

Gtr. 1 (clean)

mf

let ring let ring let ring let ring

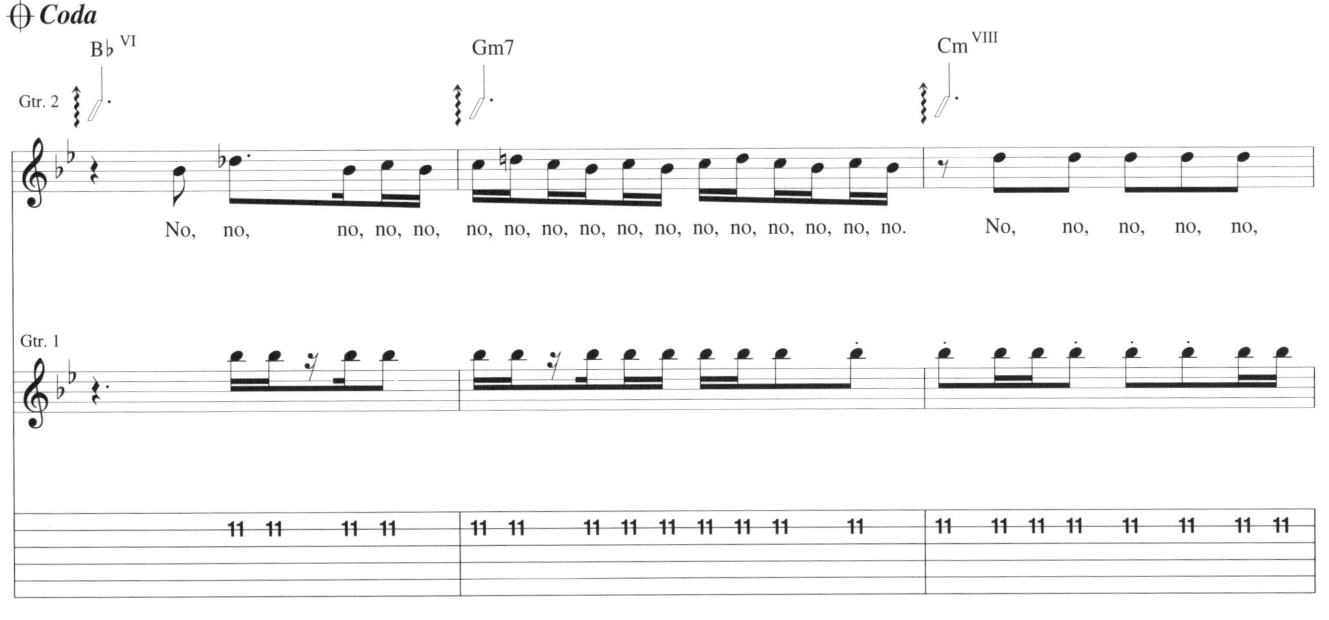
Coda
B♭ VI
Gm7
Cm VIII
Gtr. 2
No, no, no, no, no, no, no, no, no, no, no, no, no, no, no, no, no. No, no, no, no, no,
Gtr. 1

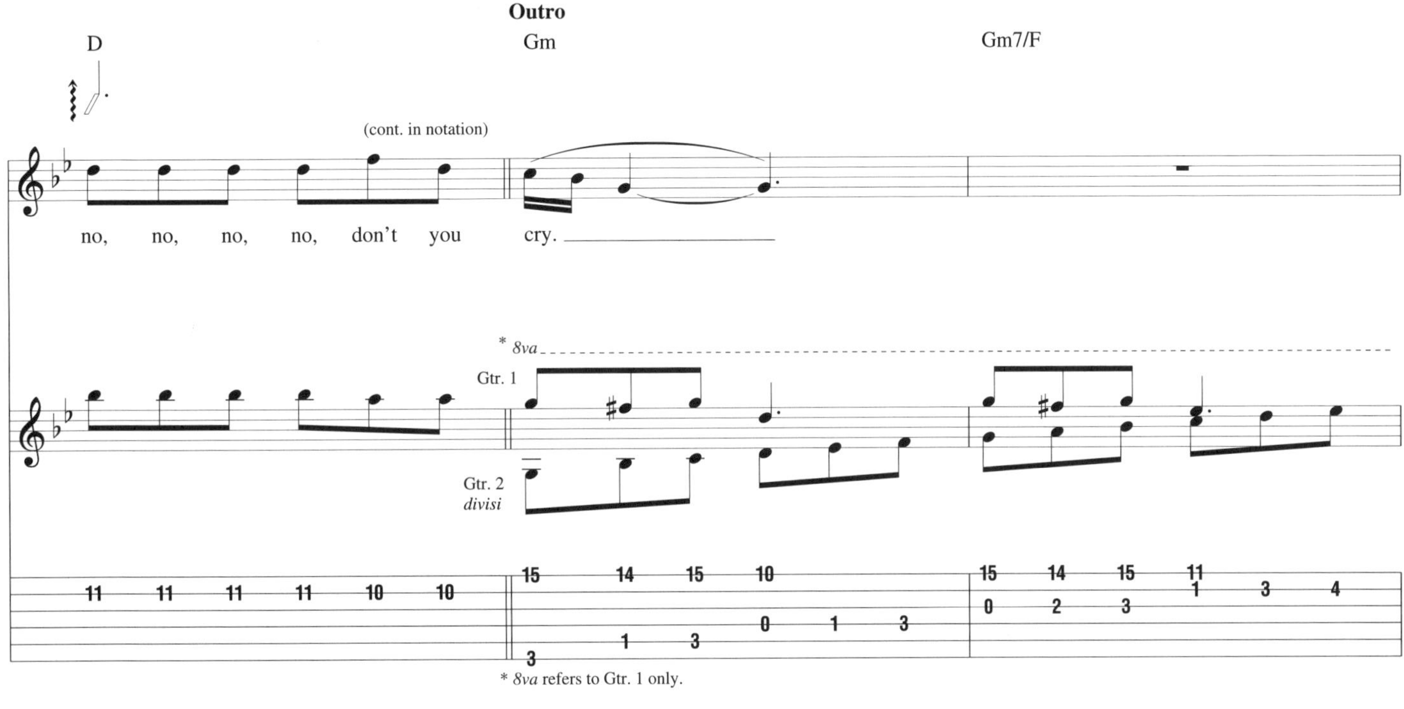
Outro
D
Gm
Gm7/F
(cont. in notation)
no, no, no, no, don't you cry.
* 8va
Gtr. 1
Gtr. 2
divisi
* 8va refers to Gtr. 1 only.

Free Time
B♭
D7
G
rit.
Oh.
8va
loco

from *I Got Dem Ol' Kozmic Blues Again Mama!*

To Love Somebody

Words and Music by Barry Gibb and Robin Gibb

F♯
C♯7
whole life to be lived with you, babe. It's what I want, oh,
-body has to ever be so blind, hon-ey, like I did. I know I was blind. Hon-ey, I
let ring
B
F♯
was to be liv-in' and lov-in' you.
tell you that I was, I was ver-y, ver-y blind.
(1.) There's a way,
(2.) Oh, but, I'm just a girl.
3. See Additional Lyrics
mf
simile on repeat
G♯m
B
oo, ev-'ry-bod-y say you can do an-y-thing,
Can't you just take a look at me and tell, tell that I live, hon-ey, I live and
full
F♯
E
ev-'ry-thing, yeah. But a-what good, what good,
I breathe for you? Don't you know I do? But a-what good, what good,

F#
C#7
hon - ey, what good can ev - er bring?
'Cause I ain't got you with my love and I can't
hon - ey, what good can ev - er do?
'Cause I ain't got you. That's all I ev - er want - ed. And I ain't
let ring
B7
find you, babe, no, I can't.
got you, babe. O - pen up and look a - round.
Chorus
F#
You don't know, you don't know what it's like,
*even 𝅘𝅥𝅮's
*played as even sixteenth notes.
C#7
no, you don't. Hon - ey no,
B
you don't know, you don't know what it's
F#
like to love an - y - bod - y.
C#7
1., 2. Oh hon', I want to talk a - bout
3. Oh hon', I want to talk a - bout
w/ pick and fingers
w/ pick and fingers

To Coda
1.
B
F♯
love and try'n to hold some-bod - y
the way I
love you, babe.
And I've been
try'n to hold you.
Oh babe, babe,
ba - by,
w/ pick & fingers
C♯
2.
F♯
lov-in' you,
babe.
love you, babe.
And I just want you to know I tried.
even ♪'s
Interlude
E
D
G♯m
F♯m
D.S. al Coda
w/ pick & fingers

Coda

F♯
yeah. But you don't know, you don't know what it's like

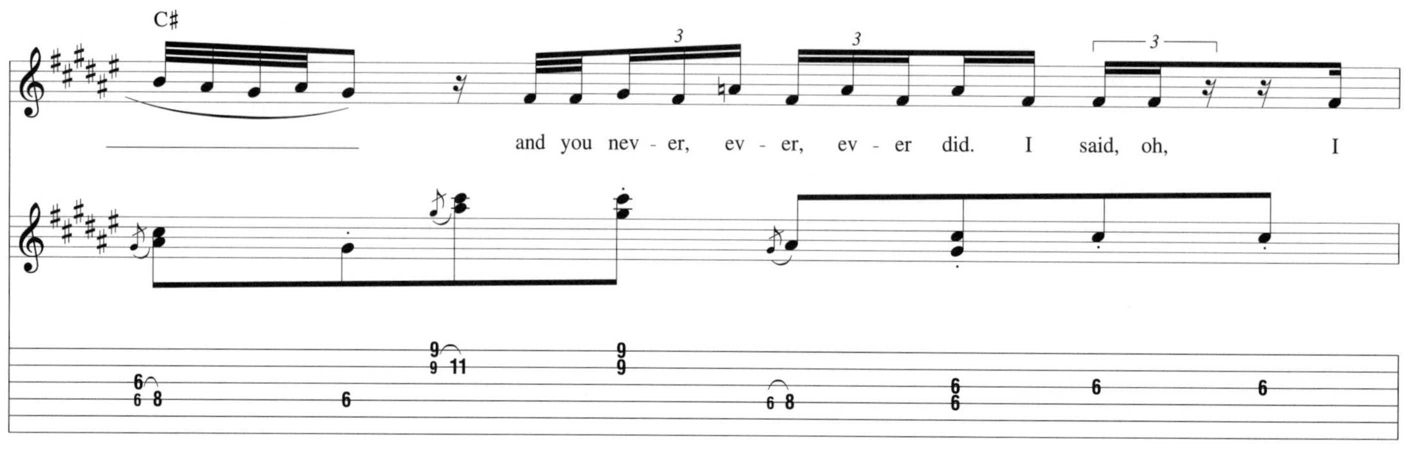
C♯
and you nev - er, ev - er, ev - er did. I said, oh, I

B
try to throw my love a - round and, and I try to help you, dar - lin',
even 𝅘𝅥𝅮's
w/ pick & fingers

F♯
but you nev - er, ev - er. No, you nev - er, ev - er.

Additional Lyrics

3. Oh, I know that there's a way.
'Cause everybody came to me one time and said,
"Honey, you can do anything, every little thing."
And I think I can.
Oh, but what good, what good.
Honey, what ugly good can it ever, ever bring?
'Cause I can't find you with my love,
And I can't find you, babe,
Oh honey, where?

from *Cheap Thrills*

Turtle Blues

Words and Music by Janis Joplin

5th time, To Coda
E5
E6
E7
E6
B7
I just cheats him like I wants to;
did. So I said, "Hon', I want the sun-shine."
A7
E
E7/D
C#°7
Am/C
I nev-er cheats, oh, honey, like I should.
He'll take the stars out of the night. And come when I give 'em to you, babe, 'cause I want 'em
1., 4.
2.
3.
B7
2. Oh, Lord, I right now.
Yeah, oh, go on.
Guitar Solo
*Gtr. 2: w/ Rhy. Fig. 1
A5
A6
A7
Gtr. 1
1/4
*acous; mf

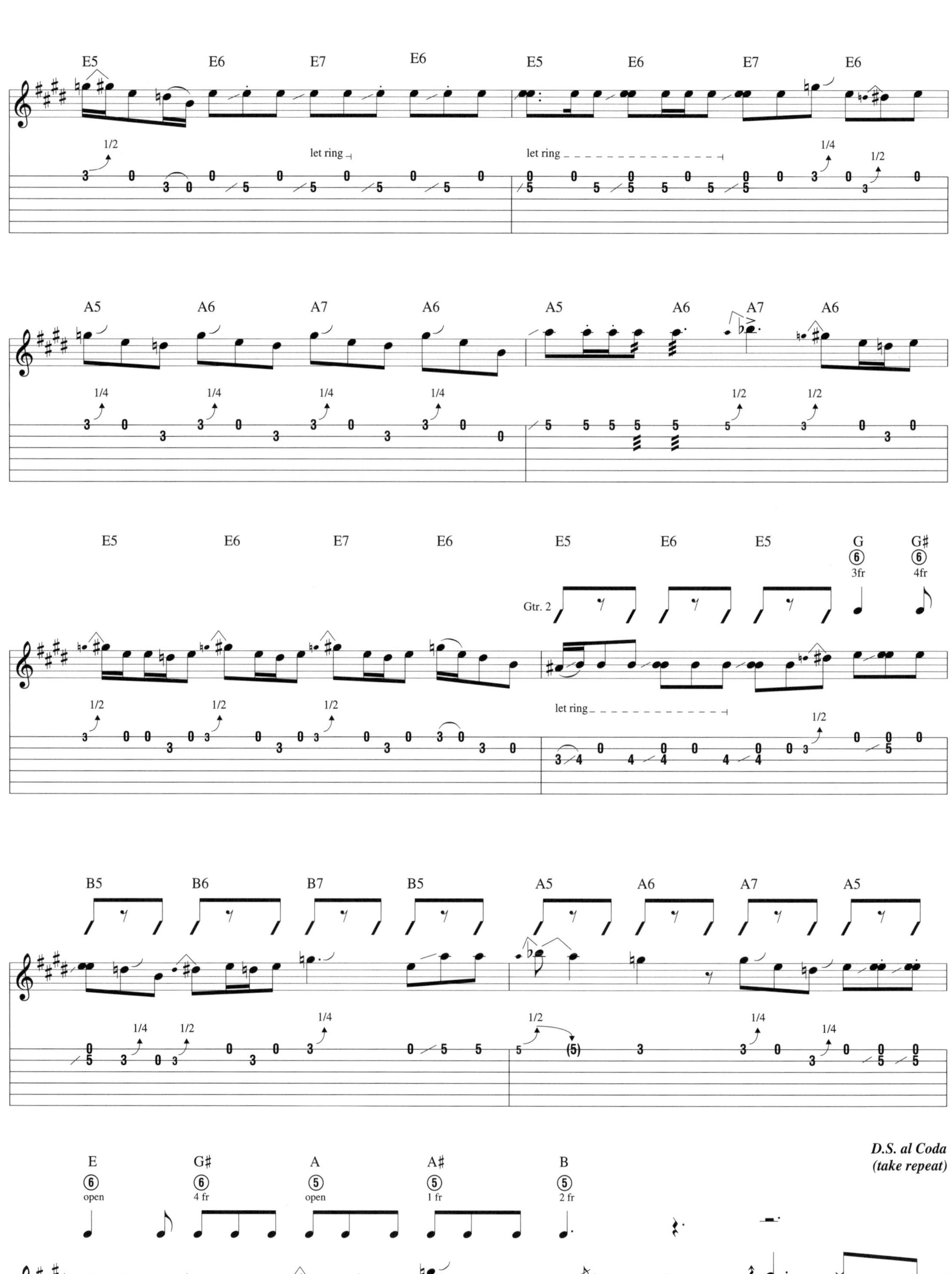
E5
E6
E7
E6
E5
E6
E7
E6
let ring
let ring
A5
A6
A7
A6
A5
A6
A7
A6
E5
E6
E7
E6
E5
E6
E5
G
G♯
Gtr. 2
let ring
B5
B6
B7
B5
A5
A6
A7
A5
E
G♯
A
A♯
B
open
4 fr
open
1 fr
2 fr
let ring
D.S. al Coda
(take repeat)

𝄌 *Coda*

Additional Lyrics

3. I ain't the kind of woman
   Who'd make your life a bed of ease.
   No, no, no, no, no, no, no, no, no.
   I'm not the kind of woman, no,
   To make your life a bed of ease.
   Yeah, but if you, if you just wanna go out drinkin', honey,
   Won't you invite me along, please?
   Oh, I'd be so good to you, babe. Yeah, oh, go on.

4. I guess I'm just like a turtle,
   That's hidin' underneath it's horny shell.
   Whoa, whoa, oh, yeah, like a turtle,
   Hidin' underneath it's horny shell.
   Don't you know I'm very well protected,
   I know this goddamn life too well.

5. Oh, don't call me mean; you could call me evil, yeah, yeah.
   I've been called much worse off things, I have.
   Oh, don't you know, yeah.
   Call me mean or call me evil.
   I've been called much worse off things, off things, right.
   Yeah, but I'm gonna take good care of Janis, yeah.
   Honey, no one gonna dog me down, alright.
   Yeah, yeah.

from *Janis*

What Good Can Drinkin' Do?

Words and Music by Janis Joplin

N.C.
B7
E
A7
drink all night, but the next day I still feel blue.
1/4
Verse
E
B7
E
A7
1. There's a glass on the ta - ble; they say it's gon - na ease all my pain.
2. Give me whis - key, give me bour - bon, give me gin.
3., 4. See Additional Lyrics
w/ thumbpick & fingers
simile on repeats
E7
A7
Now there's a glass on the ta - ble; they
Oh, give me whis - key,

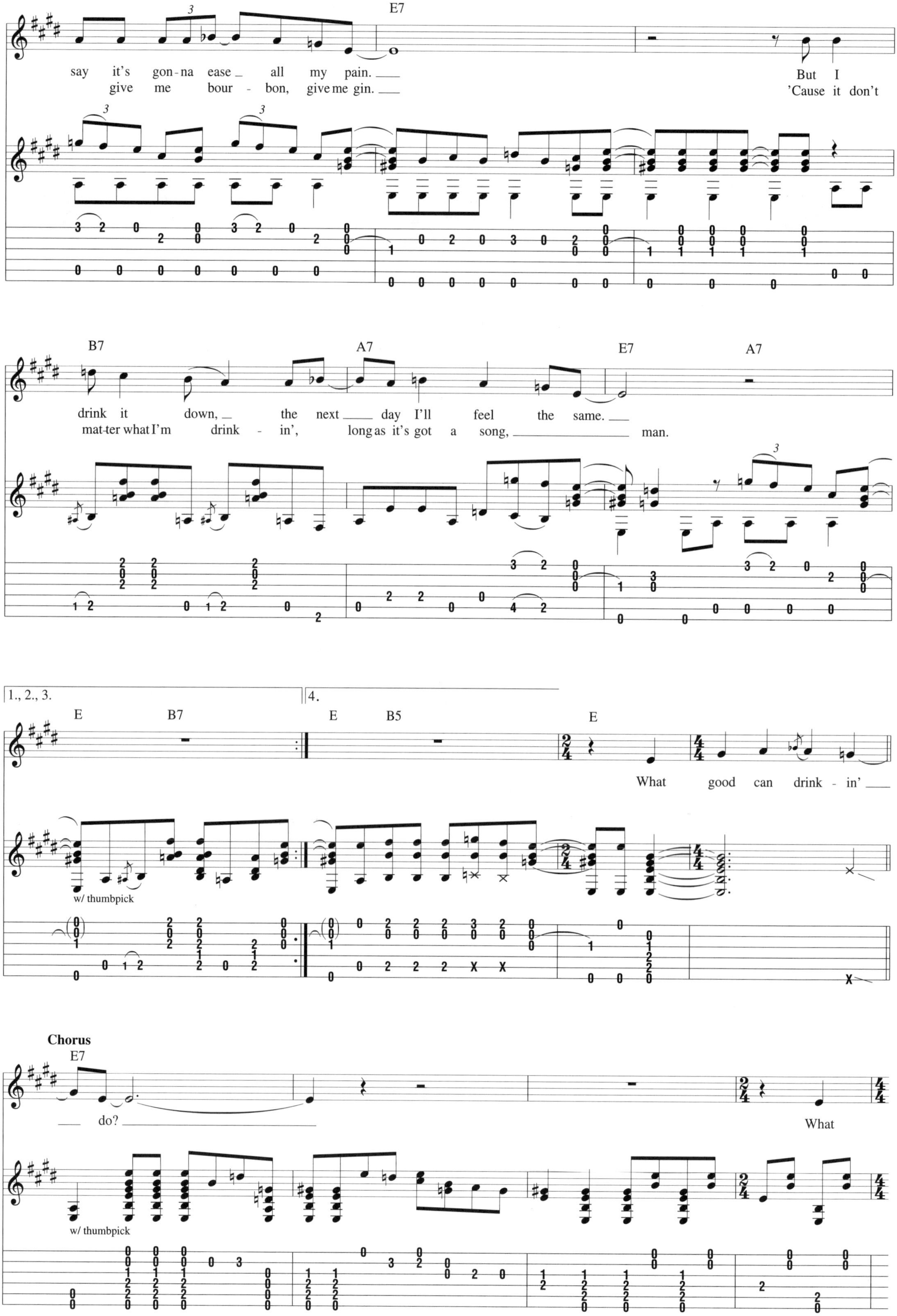

E7

say it's gon-na ease _ all my pain. ___ But I
give me bour - bon, give me gin. ___ 'Cause it don't

B7 A7 E7 A7

drink it down, _ the next ___ day I'll feel the same. ___
mat-ter what I'm drink - in', long as it's got a song, ___ man.

1., 2., 3.
E B7

w/ thumbpick

4.
E B5 E

What good can drink - in' ___

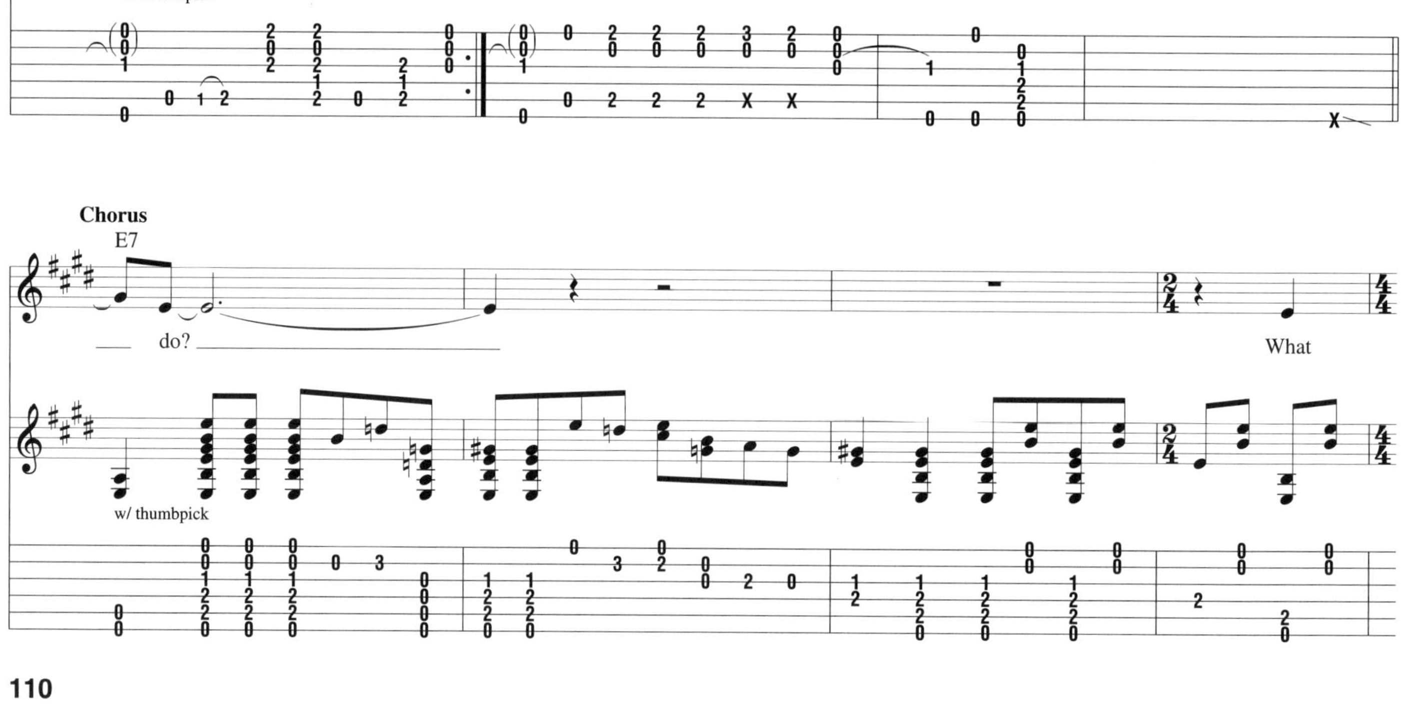

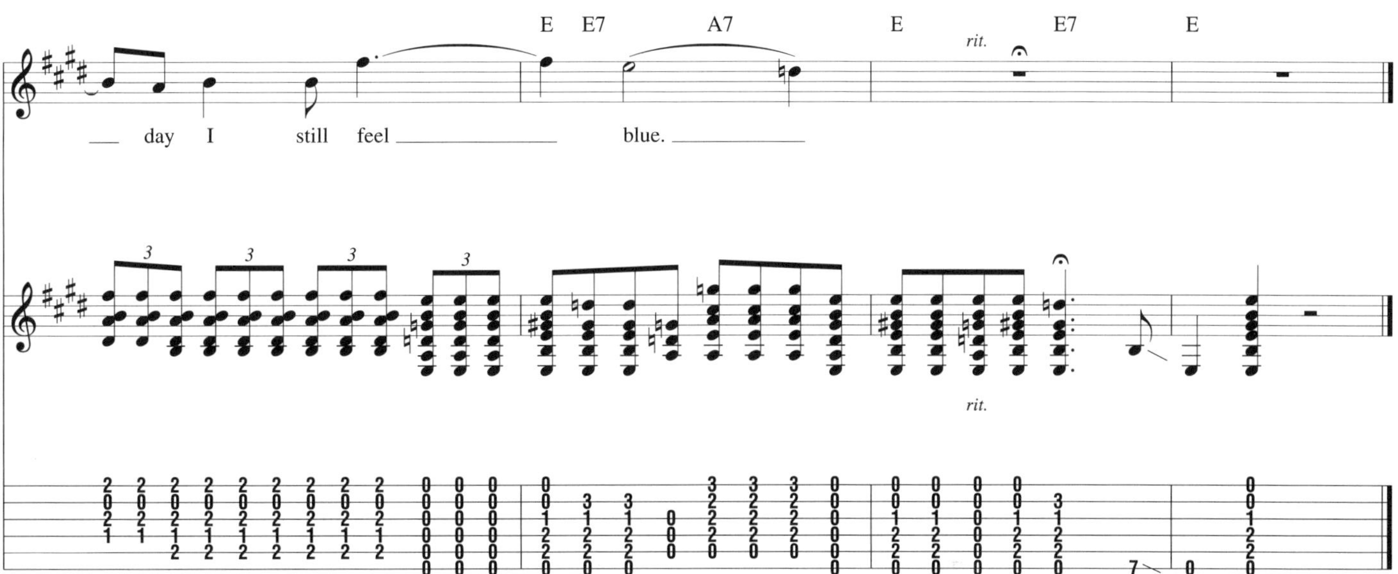

Additional Lyrics

3. Start drinkin' Friday,
I start drinkin' Friday night.
You know, I start drinkin' Friday,
Start drinkin' Friday night.
But then I wake up on Sunday,
Child, babe, nothin's right.

4. My man, he left me,
Child, he left me here.
Yeah, my good man left me,
Went away and left me here.
I'm feelin' like a dog,
Just give me another glass of beer.

Guitar Notation Legend

Guitar Music can be notated three different ways: on a *musical staff*, in *tablature*, and in *rhythm slashes*.

RHYTHM SLASHES are written above the staff. Strum chords in the rhythm indicated. Use the chord diagrams found at the top of the first page of the transcription for the appropriate chord voicings. Round noteheads indicate single notes.

THE MUSICAL STAFF shows pitches and rhythms and is divided by bar lines into measures. Pitches are named after the first seven letters of the alphabet.

TABLATURE graphically represents the guitar fingerboard. Each horizontal line represents a string, and each number represents a fret.

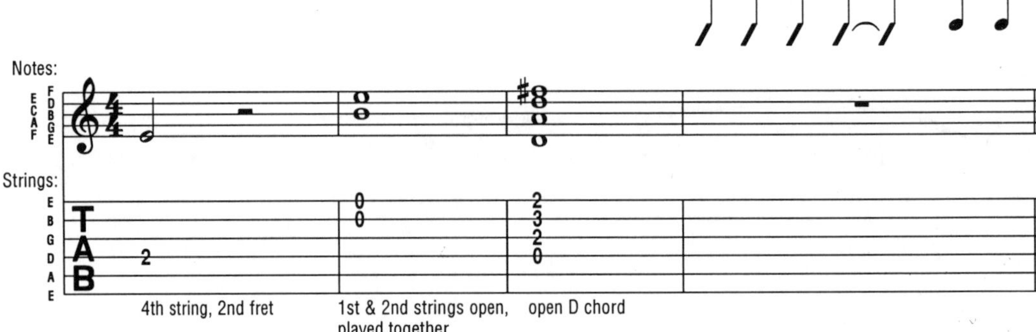

HALF-STEP BEND: Strike the note and bend up 1/2 step.

WHOLE-STEP BEND: Strike the note and bend up one step.

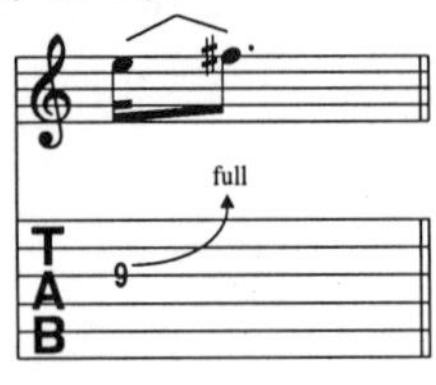

GRACE NOTE BEND: Strike the note and bend up as indicated. The first note does not take up any time.

SLIGHT (MICROTONE) BEND: Strike the note and bend up 1/4 step.

BEND AND RELEASE: Strike the note and bend up as indicated, then release back to the original note. Only the first note is struck.

PRE-BEND: Bend the note as indicated, then strike it.

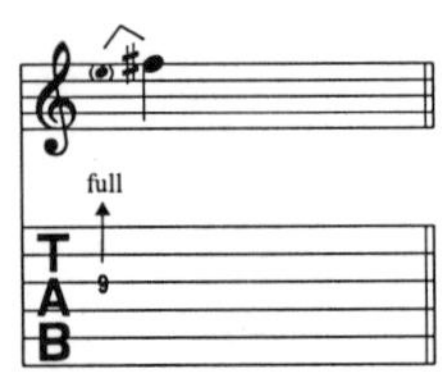

VIBRATO: The string is vibrated by rapidly bending and releasing the note with the fretting hand.

WIDE VIBRATO: The pitch is varied to a greater degree by vibrating with the fretting hand.

HAMMER-ON: Strike the first (lower) note with one finger, then sound the higher note (on the same string) with another finger by fretting it without picking.

PULL-OFF: Place both fingers on the notes to be sounded. Strike the first note and without picking, pull the finger off to sound the second (lower) note.

LEGATO SLIDE: Strike the first note and then slide the same fret-hand finger up or down to the second note. The second note is not struck.

SHIFT SLIDE: Same as legato slide, except the second note is struck.

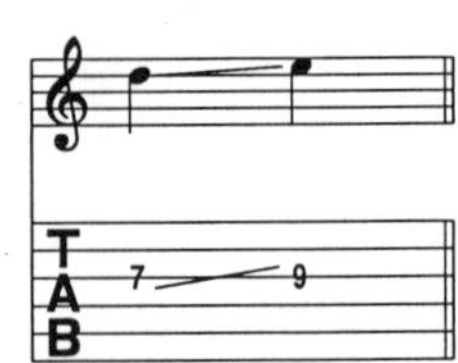

TRILL: Very rapidly alternate between the notes indicated by continuously hammering on and pulling off.

TAPPING: Hammer ("tap") the fret indicated with the pick-hand index or middle finger and pull off to the note fretted by the fret hand.

NATURAL HARMONIC: Strike the note while the fret-hand lightly touches the string directly over the fret indicated.

PINCH HARMONIC: The note is fretted normally and a harmonic is produced by adding the edge of the thumb or the tip of the index finger of the pick hand to the normal pick attack.

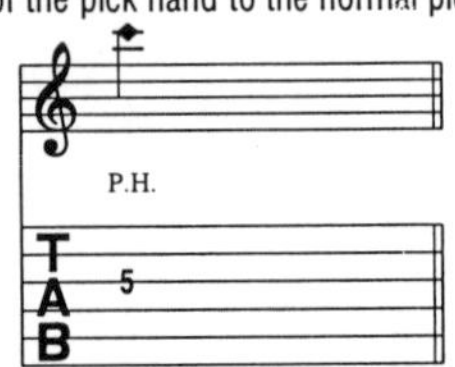

PICK SCRAPE: The edge of the pick is rubbed down (or up) the string, producing a scratchy sound.

MUFFLED STRINGS: A percussive sound is produced by laying the fret hand across the string(s) without depressing, and striking them with the pick hand.

PALM MUTING: The note is partially muted by the pick hand lightly touching the string(s) just before the bridge.

RAKE: Drag the pick across the strings indicated with a single motion.

TREMOLO PICKING: The note is picked as rapidly and continuously as possible.

VIBRATO BAR DIVE AND RETURN: The pitch of the note or chord is dropped a specified number of steps (in rhythm) then returned to the original pitch.

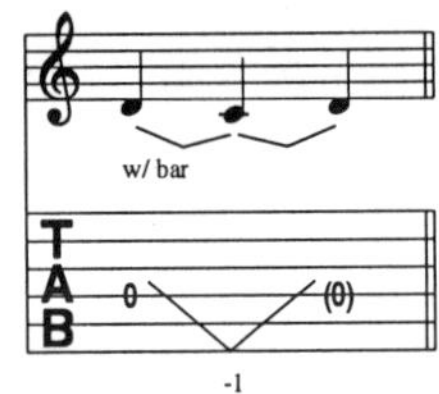

VIBRATO BAR SCOOP: Depress the bar just before striking the note, then quickly release the bar.

VIBRATO BAR DIP: Strike the note and then immediately drop a specified number of steps, then release back to the original pitch.